What Every Jew Needs to Know
About God

WHAT EVERY JEW NEEDS TO KNOW ABOUT GOD

Michael Levin

KTAV Publishing House, Inc.
Hoboken, NJ

Library of Congress Cataloging-in-Publication Data

Levin, Michael Graubart.
    What every Jew needs to know about God / by Michael Levin.
      p.   cm.
    ISBN 0-88125-537-8
    1. God (Judaism)   I. Title.
  BM610.L49   1996
  296.3'.11—dc20   96-16444
                                                     CIP

Manufactured in the United States of America
KTAV Publishing House, 900 Jefferson Street, Hoboken NJ, 07030

Table of Contents

To my wonderful friend and editor, Yaakov Elman:

There are moments in which, to use a talmudic phrase, "heaven and earth kiss . . . "
—Abraham Joshua Heschel
God in Search of Man

"[A] little boy...was playing chess with his father. The father had just set up the chessboard, and the little boy said to him, 'Why must the board always be just like that? Why couldn't we move the kings and rooks over here, and the pawns over there?' And the father answered, 'We could do those things, but then the game wouldn't be chess anymore.'"

—from *Holy Days*, by Lis Harris

1

What the Other Boys Knew

The summer after I graduated from college, I was working in New York, putting aside money to go to Israel. I wanted to study in a Jerusalem yeshiva or religious school and learn, really learn, about Judaism.

I had grown up in the suburbs and my family attended a Reform congregation. My earliest memories of Judaism, though, consisted of attending Orthodox High Holiday services with my grandparents when I was a very little boy. I loved the cantor's quavering, mournful voice—and I found myself fascinated by his hat, which looked like a large velvet crown. The services went on forever. I didn't mind, because I loved being with my grandparents, who always made a big deal about me.

I guess I always had a thing about Judaism. When I was seven, I made a little synagogue out of my building blocks and put on religious services in the den. I was the rabbi and Emily Russo, the girl who lived in the house behind ours, was my entire congregation.

In my real life, I was happy with our temple. We had a cantor with a beautiful voice and a young rabbi who loved kids. I liked our services, even if they didn't have the old-style feel of my grandparents' synagogue. There was lots of singing and the sermons weren't *too* long.

Around the time of my Bar Mitzvah, though, a funny thing happened. I won a Bible contest in my temple and I was sent to New York to compete on the regional level. I didn't do very well at the regionals, but I saw something that day that I've never forgotten.

My test, on the book of Samuel, was in English, and was multiple choice.

The other boys at my table, some of whom were wearing *yarmulkes* on their heads, had a different test. Their questions were in *Hebrew*. And they wrote essay answers. *Also* in *Hebrew*.

They knew something I didn't know.

In fact, they knew *a lot* of things I didn't know.

I guess that was the day when I made up my mind to know as much about Judaism as they did.

I thought of that moment a few years later when I was about fifteen and I was travelling around on some kind of tour with a bunch of kids from Kansas. One evening we were all just playing cards or talking and the conversation turned to religion. The kids from Kansas were all Christians and they wanted to know why Jews didn't accept Jesus Christ as the Messiah.

I felt really frustrated because I didn't know why not. But those kids with the yarmulkes—I bet *they* knew. I just knew we didn't. I wanted to give those kids a good answer. But I couldn't. The Christian kids weren't mean and they weren't trying to convert me. They just wanted an answer. I think a lot of Jewish kids go through this experience.

Not much changed in my level of Jewish knowledge until I got to college a couple of years later. I took exactly one Jewish Scriptures class. We studied the Bible—mostly Genesis and Exodus, and some of the Prophets. I didn't do very well. I got a C plus, in fact. I still wanted to learn about Judaism, but I figured I better not destroy my GPA in the process. So my interest in Judaism waned for a few more years.

This was back in the 1970s. At the time, there was this famous article in *Rolling Stone* magazine about a young woman whose brother had gone to Israel and got caught up in an Orthodox yeshiva. She went to see what had happened to him and found herself compelled, but not convinced, by the rabbis' arguments about the truth of the Torah. Her brother remained at the yeshiva; she didn't.

I saw this article in Barcelona. I was backpacking around Europe and I'd run into another guy from my college. He was thinking about going to that yeshiva to see for himself. That's where I got the idea to do the same thing.

The following June, the summer between my junior and senior year of college, I went to Israel and found a school a lot like the one in the *Rolling Stone* article. It had been created to train Jews like me, who grew up with limited Jewish education, to learn all the things those other kids knew. I made up my mind. After I graduated, I'd come to one of those schools and get the facts.

And I did. But while I was working in New York that summer, putting aside money for the trip, a very strange thing happened that briefly rocked the Jewish world.

A minister, speaking to a large convention of a particular Christian denomination, made the headlines by announcing that "God does not hear the prayers of Jews."

I remember how hurt I felt by that statement. What a thing to say! What a low blow. Of course God heard the prayers of Jews. God heard my prayers, the prayers of the other people at my temple, my grandparents' prayers, the prayers of the cantor with the velvet hat. Of course God heard the prayers of Jews.

The minister apologized for his remark, and most people forgot about it.

I went to Israel and studied Hebrew and Bible and Talmud and Jewish law for a year. I loved it, and it's been a major part of my life ever since. I may never know as much as those boys at the Bible exam. But at least I know *something*.

And yet, I could never get that minister's comment out of my head.

And then one day I realized that in a very strange way *the minister was right*.

God *didn't* hear the prayers of Jews.

But not because God discriminated against Jews, or didn't like Jews, or liked other religions better.

God didn't hear the prayers of Jews because a massive proportion of Jews *didn't pray*.

One Sabbath morning I was at services and they passed out results of a new survey. According to the survey, only eight percent of Jews attended services on a regular basis.

Eight percent. Math genius that I am, I was able to rapidly calculate that ninety-two percent of Jews did not go to services more than a few times a year.

Ninety-two percent! How could that be? How could it be that only one Jew in twelve went to synagogue at least once a month? Certainly Jews prayed outside of temple, but why was organized religion so unattractive to most Jews? I thought about this for a long time. I wondered why Jews express their Judaism in a thousand different ways—politically, culturally, gastronomically—but not religiously.

What does praying to God mean? If I'm going to pray, I'm essentially saying the following:

1) God exists. 2) God cares about me enough to listen to my prayers. 3) There is some purpose to praying. 4) My prayers might get answered.

And if you consider these four points, it's instantly obvious why so many Jews don't pray, or don't pray regularly, or don't come to a religious service to pray with others.

First, we just survived the Holocaust. Where was God? Did God listen to the prayers of Jews back then?

Second, the world is a hideous mess. Wars, disease, poverty: maybe God existed at one time. But lately?

Third, prayer somehow feels like a thing that other religions do. Christians and Moslems pray. They go to church, or the mosque, and have one-to-one relationships with God. What do we Jews do? We don't so much *pray* as we *attend* services. Why? Because our families expect us to.

I remember one year—I was probably around fifteen—and I didn't want to go to Yom Kippur services. My parents nearly killed me.

Fourth, we don't learn much about prayer. Maybe the boys with the yarmulkes were taught about prayer—about the how-to aspects of it. About how you're supposed to feel, about what words to say, about how to attune yourself to something invisible and vast and omnipresent. It's been a few years now, obviously, but when

I think about my Sunday School and Hebrew School education, I remember learning about the State of Israel, the Holocaust, and the Bible. We didn't learn much about prayer, or about God, for that matter.

Well, here I am, not a scholar, not a professor, not an expert. I'm a Jew who happens to believe that God exists, that God cares enough about me to listen to my prayers, that there is some purpose to praying, and that my prayers do get answered.

Whenever I go to a bookstore, I can't help but notice that the sections on Spirituality, New Age, and Religion are crammed with books about how to connect with something outside of ourselves. And a lot of people flipping through those books look Jewish.

I don't blame any Jew who doesn't pray today. I was fortunate enough to see Judaism "on the inside" and I have been blessed with just enough knowledge to make the Jewish concept of God real and alive to me. My suspicion is that a lot of Jews wish they had a deeper understanding, but not only of how to celebrate this holiday or how to observe this particular custom.

I think a lot of Jews are curious about God.

If their Jewish education was anything like mine, they probably didn't get answers to a lot of important questions.

Maybe this book can help.

2

"Bored, Shnorred, and Ignored"

All too often, when Jews go to services, looking for God, tradition, comfort, or spiritual release, something bad happens. They feel bored, shnorred, and ignored.

Bored because the service is dull or incomprehensible or both. It doesn't come close to touching that place inside us where we feel awe and wonder at the miracle of our existence in the universe. We go, rightly expecting some sort of spiritual "high"—but we usually don't get it.

Shnorred—a Yiddish word referring to begging or panhandling. Most Jews attend services on the High Holy Days, which, to our dismay, have become the High Fundraising Days and the High Giving of Jewish Guilt Days.

Ignored because synagogues and temples often fail to meet the spiritual, educational, and religious needs of their members. If they were doing a better job, they would attract more than eight percent of us on a regular basis. Given that deadly combination of bored, shnorred, and ignored, why would anyone go back?

And yet . . .

We know that to be Jewish means something greater than feeling proud of the State of Israel, or remembering the Holocaust, or writing checks to Jewish philanthropies.

We know that Jewishness implies a special relationship of some sort with God. (A friend of mine says, "Even if we're not the Chosen People, we're definitely an option.) But our Jewish educations, if we had any at all—and, according to one study, about forty percent of us had none whatsoever[1]—were so timid when it came to theology that we aren't even sure if God exists now, or if there ever was a God.

How is it possible that a people could have survived for so long without a country, without a political structure, without a Vatican-like chief religious authority; a people despised, envied, murdered, and expelled from virtually every country it called home. How could a people like that manage to avoid total extinction?

And how could that people survive for so long, only to end up with religious services and religious education so insubstantial as to drive away ninety-two percent of its members? Why, when it comes to religion, do nine out of ten of us feel alienated, unwanted, and disconnected?

What went wrong?

Jews are no different from anyone else. We have the same questions about life that everyone else has.

We want to know whether life has a purpose.

We want to know how we are supposed to behave.

We want to know why the world exists.

We want to know whether there is a God and who or what God is.

We want to know whether God has any expectations of us, and if so, how we are supposed to go about fulfilling those expectations.

We also want to know how the world was created.

We want to know what, if anything, happens after we die.

We want to know if there really is a heaven or a hell, and how you earn one and avoid the other.

We want to know why good people may suffer while evildoers flourish.

We want to know what to tell the children.

And we want to know the answer to the most important question of all: "Why am I here?"

Judaism's main problem today is that it has forgotten its central purpose: to give Jews answers to these questions. Other religions still try to answer the ultimate questions. While their adherents may not always like the answers they get, the other religions don't have a problem of ninety-two percent nonattendance.

It's hard for a religion to succeed if it doesn't address real life-and-death issues of purpose and meaning and judgment and afterlife and what to tell the children.

For four thousand years, Judaism had a "mission statement." Its mission: teach its members to understand, appreciate, and serve God while still enjoying life and life's pleasures, and teach them to be good people, responsible for the welfare of their families and their society. The prophet Micah summed up the Jewish mission statement this way: "What does God want from you, other than to do justly, love mercy, and walk humbly with your God?"[2] If you could travel in time to any moment in history over the last four thousand years, and asked the Jews you met what Judaism meant to them, they would tell you pretty much the same thing: a way of life centered on a close relationship with God.

For four thousand years, Jews actually had a firm idea of God. God was one, not many. God was loving, caring, and present. God was enormous, beyond the scope of human understanding; yet God sought to have a bond with people. God listened when you spoke, when you prayed, when you cried out. God was everywhere in the universe, and God was inside us. God was a parent, a ruler, a best friend, a constant companion. God was definite and real. For Jews, God was an eternal, living, compassionate presence.

Jews believed in God's existence even though they were not always happy about the state of the world. They considered their connection to God, in many ways, their most valuable possession. They never let go of their idea of God regardless of poverty, pogroms, expulsions, and even genocide.

For nineteen hundred years, from the destruction of the Second Temple in Jerusalem until the foundation of the modern State of Israel, Jews were a people without a country. Exiled from our land, we lived among others who often hated us because we would not worship God the way they did. They saw our adherence to our traditions as a threat to the validity of their beliefs. Over and over, in century after century, Jews were offered the same choices: conversion, exile, or death. If a close relationship with God was the best thing about being Jewish, the anti-Semitism our relationship with God provoked was the worst.

Why, over history, have people often hated Jews? According to historian Paul Johnson, anti-Jewishness dates back to the middle of the first century B.C.E. He sets forth five reasons: Jews would not acknowledge other peoples' gods; circumcision set Jews apart; laws of diet and cleanliness separated Jews and non-Jews; avoiding intermarriage made Jews seem "misanthropic";

and Jews refused to practice emperor-worship in Rome.[3] Later, we committed the "crime" of knowing about Christianity but not accepting it.[4]

It's impossible for a people to suffer two thousand years of hatred, culminating in the Holocaust, without buying into that hatred. On some level, we came to believe that there was something hateful about being a Jew. If people despised us so much, we decided, something about us must be despicable. In psychological terms, "self-hating" Jews are simply Jews who have accepted or internalized some of the hatred the world has had for us.

No one wants to feel hated.

Somewhere in our collective Jewish subconscious arose the idea that if only we could eliminate whatever it is inside us that provokes the rest of the world to hate us, we could at last find some peace. In many ways, the last century and a half of Jewish history has been a series of attempts to eliminate the aspects of Jewishness that we believe cause others to hate us.

And the main aspect of Jewishness is the way we worship God.

Think about it: Jews were hated and persecuted because we didn't worship God the way others did. So we thought we could make a deal: if we abandoned our close relationship with God, the Gentile world might stop hating and persecuting us. Unfortunately, one Holocaust and six million Jewish souls later, we found that the strategy didn't work. And what are we left with? A people ninety-two percent of whom feel estranged from God, while anti-Semitism continues to flourish. In short, we have the worst of both worlds. We threw away our spiritual moorings and we still bear the burden of anti-Semitism. How did we get into this predicament?

The major turning point in modern Jewish history was not the Holocaust or the creation of the modern State of Israel. It was the combination of events in the late eighteenth century that led to the lowering of the ghetto walls in European communities and the loosening of restrictions on Jewish participation in business, culture, education, and politics. New forms of Judaism emerged to meet the changing times. For many Jews, the traditional beliefs and practices did not fit well with their new lives. Reform and Conservative Judaism were born, seeking to harmonize traditional Jewish values with the new roles of Jews in a changing world.

The traditionally-minded, of course, were shocked by these new approaches to Judaism. But the architects of the new groups argued that Judaism had always changed—and they were right. They could point to a midrash, a thousand-year-old rabbinical story, recounting that Moses visited the study hall of Rabbi Akiva, who lived perhaps twelve hundred years after the Exodus. According to the story, Moses realized that he did not understand *a single word* of what was being said about the Torah he had received from God on Mount Sinai!

And yet, the story implied, the *evolution* of Judaism from desert times to modern times was a perfectly acceptable thing.

But Judaism had never changed so suddenly, the traditionalists believed. And never had so many traditions, practices, and prayers been trimmed away.

These radically new forms of Judaism rapidly took root across Germany and then made their way to the rest of Europe and the United States. Liberal Jewish congregations garbed their rabbis in black Lutheran robes, making them look like Christian ministers. They added organs to their temples, just as churches and cathedrals had organs. Jewish law had always forbidden musical instruments at Sabbath services, as a mourning custom. The absence of music served as a reminder to the faithful of the destruction of the main Temple in Jerusalem, where musical services accompanied divine worship all day long.

The Reform Jews of nineteenth century Europe also stopped praying in Hebrew, the holy tongue that had served to unite Jews, and Jewish prayer, over the centuries and across the continents. They prayed instead in the local language of the country—German, or French, or Italian, or English. For the first time in several thousand years, educating Jewish children no longer meant teaching them to read, pray, and speak in their ancient language.

When it came to the prayers themselves, the liberal Jews did not translate them verbatim. They considered themselves rationalists, men and women who believed that if something did not make rational sense, or seemed disloyal to their European home country, it had to be removed. And so they eliminated everything that struck them as irrational.

Now, faith means believing in something even though you cannot prove it rationally. And so, with rationality the test, the Jewish prayer book required a lot of revamping. Since the reformers in Frankfort and Hanover felt themselves to be good German citizens and wanted to be accepted as such, how could they pray for a redeemer to take them from Germany? Out, therefore, went references to the Messiah, an idea Jews had held dear for several thousand years.

Gone also were the rules restricting activity on the Sabbath day. The idea that a God had created the world or "rested" when finished seemed not just irrational but inconvenient. How could one do business with Gentiles if one closed shop on Saturday? And gone were the laws regarding kosher food, for the same two reasons: they were irrational, and they interfered with business and social contacts with Gentiles.

Today we do not dress the way German Jews dressed in the early nineteenth century. We do not adhere to their diet, language, or customs. We do not entertain ourselves or travel as they did. And we hardly consider Germany the best home the Jewish people have ever known.

And yet. Those enormous nineteenth century changes in Judaism anticipated to a remarkable degree the way the majority of Jews today think about God, religion, and Judaism—to the extent that they think about these things at all. Many Jews today pray, or don't pray, the way those early nineteenth-century Jews prayed; many believe what they believed, and ignore everything in Judaism that they ignored.

The initial mass appeal of Reform Judaism was that it made it possible for us to be Jews unobtrusively. It enabled us to avoid the spiritual aspects of our Jewishness that triggered such blinding rage in Gentiles—and in ourselves. At last we could be Jews the way Christians were Christians. And we thought, if we're not *doing* the things that make us seem different, no one will hate us anymore.

Of course, no one asked whether a Jew was Reform or Conservative or Orthodox in the death camps. The Nazis were indifferent to such distinctions. This is the great tragedy: we surrendered much of our closeness to God in hopes of receiving acceptance from the Gentile world, but the strategy in many important ways didn't work.

Today, half a century after the Holocaust, we are still quiet about our Judaism. We limit our show of Jewishness to, perhaps, a large coffee-table-size book about the State of Israel in our living rooms, a mezuzah on the front door, quiet contributions to Jewish organizations and brief, bored appearances at High Holiday services that often appear to have more to do with fundraising and satisfying our parents than with spirituality. Perhaps we march in a rally or a parade, or wear a Star of David around our necks—a direct imitation of Christians wearing crosses, incidentally. Yet when we're around Gentiles, we often discreetly tuck them away.

We don't admit it often, but even today we still live in fear of a quieter form of anti-Semitism. It lingers like a low-grade fever in the form of hate letters to Jews, swastikas occasionally spray-painted on Jewish tombstones, or subtle or blatant discrimination in certain business firms, social clubs, and schools.

We sense that neither we nor our children should appear "too Jewish," and although we cannot define exactly what "too Jewish" means, we know it has to do with being too loud or too pushy or too interested in driving a bargain. What Christian parent tells a Christian child to avoid being "too Christian"? Christians publicly proclaim their Christianity with an openness and a happiness and a sense of pride that most of us couldn't imagine feeling about Jewishness.

But we're entitled to that feeling of complete pride. We deserve to feel it.

The basic idea of this book is that Jews once had a passionate, satisfying, clear, and joyous relationship with God. To be Jewish meant to feel connected with God. But today, we have to ask ourselves why so few Jews go to services, educate their children about Judaism, or marry other Jews. We have to ask ourselves why the whole thing means so little to us. My belief, based on my experience growing up in secular Jewish society and my exposure, from my college years on, to traditional Jewish beliefs and practices, is that Jews would feel a lot more connected to Judaism if they knew more about the Jewish conception of God. And that's what this book is about.

Today, most Jews view Judaism as a religion without a core. They feel that it cannot meet their spiritual needs. I think the fault is not in Judaism; I think most Jews simply haven't been exposed to the real core of spirituality *in* Judaism. And that core is the way we have related, for thousands of years, to God.

We're educated people and we read the papers, and in today's world, God seems to have fallen into the wrong hands. Those who publicly claim an intimate relationship with God are often frightening. They are Moonies, marrying seventeen thousand strangers to one another at one time. They are television and radio evangelists, the crass manipulating the vulnerable. They are people with a strange look in their eyes who accost you in airports and public places. They have usurped God. The Lord of Hosts...is their hostage.

Moreover, some of the greatest influences on modern thought happen to be the work of Jews who had no use for theology or God. Karl Marx told the world that religion was the opiate of the masses. Jews believed him. (And anti-Semites could then go around and accuse us of being Communists.)

After Marx came Sigmund Freud, who wrote that the Bible contained nothing but childish fantasies, that God was "an illusion that mature men and women should lay aside."[5] For decades, psychiatrists and therapists saw it as their role to free individuals from the need for an ultimate parent figure in the form of God. Marx and Freud told us to stop believing in God, and we obeyed.

Other influences against a Jewish sense of God in one's daily life are more subtle. We have accepted the false ideas that the "Old Testament God" was a punishing God, and that only other faiths, Christianity and Buddhism especially, have a God of love. Traditionally, Jews have called their Scriptures the *Tanakh*, or in English the Hebrew Bible, not the "Old Testament." The "Old Testament" is a Christian name for a Jewish book. We never asked to have our holiest book renamed with a title that suggests that it's out of date. Now, Christians have every right to call the Bible anything they want.

But Jews who use the term "Old Testament" are buying into a Christian renaming of a Jewish holy book.

And if you actually *read* the Hebrew Bible, you find God just as loving as in the Christian understanding of God. The one-dimensional notion of a vindictive Old Testament God is not a Jewish concept. So we don't have to accept other, outside interpretations of our God and our Bible as (dare I say it) "gospel truth."

God gets a bad rap in other ways as well. In our secular culture, only floods, fires, earthquakes, and other disasters are referred to as "acts of God." But if these are acts of God, who gets the credit for rainbows, flowers, autumn leaves, the miracle of birth, and all sorts of other good things? Hmm?

Christian authors address such concerns. Their bestselling works offer readers ways to have a dynamic relationship with God. Well-known Christian inspirational books have upbeat, optimistic titles like *The Power of Positive Thinking, The Sermon on the Mount, You Can If You Think You Can, The Richest Man on Earth,* and *The Be-Happy Attitudes.* The only Jewish inspirational book in the last twenty years to attract a massive readership? *When Bad Things Happen to Good People.*

But the main reason why so many Jews today have no use for God is the Holocaust. If there is a God—a loving God—how could the Holocaust ever have happened? This is an extremely important question, and we will consider it in depth in the next chapter.

In short, we Jews do not see ourselves as having a close relationship with a loving God. And that explains why, week after week, ninety-two percent of us avoid synagogues and temples. Yet something inside us craves answers to the questions listed above. We pack the Spirituality and New Age sections of bookstores and libraries. We go to therapists, meditation teachers, retreats, even churches, trying to get some sense of what life is all about. The only place we never think to look for a sense of God and the meaning of life is in Judaism itself.

We Jews have not lost our need to express our spirituality, our craving to understand our place in the world, and our desire to make contact with the Being or force that created the world. We simply have had our Jewish means to do so, stripped away. Jews ache for some idea of how to understand whether there is a God and what our individual and collective relationship to God could be. That's our topic. Let's get going.

3

"God Was Here, But He Went Home Early"

Atheists believe that God does not exist. Agnostics do not know whether God exists. Woody Allen once said that "An atheist married an agnostic, and they couldn't agree how not to bring up the children." Seriously, a lot of people today believe one or more of the following things:

1) There never was a God.

2) There was a God once, but not now. (The title of this chapter is the title of a short story by Irwin Shaw.)

3) God can't be loving—look at the way the world is.

People who do not believe in the existence of God tend to hold that position for one or both of two reasons. Reason one: if there were a God, where is the justice when good people in our lives—family, friends—suffer, and bad people get away with doing bad things?

Reason two: if there were a God, how could that God permit a world of war and cruelty?

It's really the same question. The only difference is the scale of the tragedy—whether it's personal or world-wide.

We all have known decent people, adults and children, who died before their time. What kind of God creates a world where the good die young? Where is the justice? And we all see the results on television or in the newspapers of the inexorable cruelty that human beings seemingly delight in inflicting on each other—more often than not, alas, in God's name. Where is the peace that we would expect from a loving God?

This is the age-old dilemma that the sages of the Talmud expressed, with their usual terseness, in the phrase *tzaddik v'ra lo*, a righteous person to whom bad happens. Add to this problem yet another stumbling block when it comes to accepting the existence of God: we have no proof.

Sometimes it seems that all the evidence as to whether God exists suggests that the answer is no.

There might not have been drive-by shootings or AIDS epidemics or nuclear weapons in biblical days, but even a cursory glance at the Bible suggests that the world of ancient Israel was as violent as ours. And although we read that Moses lived for a hundred and twenty years, the very fact that the Bible considers this noteworthy indicates that not everyone enjoyed such a long and healthy lifespan. Given that the Jews of the biblical and talmudic eras witnessed violence, illness, and inexplicable death, how on earth did *they* come to accept the idea of a loving God?

Any talk about a personal relationship with God, the central theme of this book, means nothing until we come up with at least minimally satisfying answers to the problem of how evil, cruelty, war, poverty, and deprivation could exist in a world created by a God who might be trusted, a God worthy of our attention and prayers.

I am no philosopher. But I had to make peace with this matter in my own life, and at a very early age.

My own Jewish background actually includes Reform, Conservative, and Orthodox Judaism. My father's parents were active in their Conservative temple for decades. My mother's parents came from nonpracticing Orthodox households in Poland. Their parents—my great-grandparents—were Chortkeve Hasidim, members of a small Hasidic group named for the town where their leader, or rebbe, settled.

I mentioned earlier that when I was a little boy, I used to accompany my mother's parents to High Holiday services at their Orthodox synagogue in Manhattan. I used to stand between my grandfather and one of his friends, swaying giants in white prayer shawls to my four-year-old eyes, and I would pretend I could follow the Hebrew letters in the prayer book. After Yom Kippur, the Day of Atonement, ended, I was allowed to sit next to my grandfather as he broke his fast, so long as I didn't talk to him while he was eating. And oh, how he ate, after those fast days.

I once heard that our religious sensibilities are fixed by age four. If that's true, I suppose it happened on the High Holidays at Congregation Ohab Zedek in New York, more than thirty years ago, that I formulated my idea of God as an approachable source of distant mystery. When I was that little boy, God was in the quavering, otherworldly tenor of the cantor with the velvet hat: a serious mystery, a presence, something real. If God weren't real, why would my grandfather, a reasonable man, and all his friends, give up a day of work and not eat? There *had* to be a God. Otherwise all these people wouldn't spend the whole day praying.

My concept of God as a loving being took a terrible beating just after my tenth birthday. My grandfather, who escaped the Holocaust with his immediate family by being smuggled into Spain in a hay wagon, who taught me soccer because he played that game as a boy in Sunok, Poland, my grandfather who took me to his Orthodox synagogue to pray in a mysterious, baleful, painfully exquisite tongue, my loving grandfather was murdered in a hold-up while on a business trip to Chicago.

Devastated, I made a sign out of shirt cardboard announcing that "God is dead." Now, where did a ten-year-old Jewish boy get in his head Friedrich Nietzsche's idea that God had died? This illustrates the degree to which we Jews, even as children, find ourselves imbued with non-Jewish notions. When you were ten, did St. Peter guard the pearly gates in your mind's-eye view of heaven? Did a devil with a pitchfork punish the evil in fiery hell? Then you, too, were influenced by non-Jewish ideas from a very early age.

My "God is dead" sign shocked our next-door neighbors, devout Christians. My parents probably asked me to put it away, at least while we were sitting *shiva*, spending days at home accepting visitors during the initial period of mourning.

God?

It took me many years to reconcile myself to God after that loss and after the subsequent loss of my beloved grandmother, who died of cancer that was really a metastasized broken heart.

As a ten-year-old I had no tools to understand the loss of my grandfather. Today I do, and I want to share them with you.

One of the key tenets of Judaism is the idea of free will—the idea that God does not interfere with the actions of human beings. Here is how Deuteronomy, the fifth book of the Bible, puts it: "I set before you this day the choice of doing good or doing evil."[6] In other words, you get free will.

The opposite of free will is a world where people have no choices; where we live, essentially, like plants—growing in a fixed manner in a fixed place, contributing in some small way to the ecosystem, but not with any choice in the matter. Or we might live like animals, operating on instinct, not conscience.

Free will means that if we want to do something terrible to someone else, God will not stop us. Free will gives us the chance to create life—and to take it away. In other words, the idea of free will allows for tragedy to happen.

In Jewish thought, free will coexists uneasily with the idea of foreknowledge, which means that God knows in advance which choice we are going to make, whether we will choose to do the right thing or the wrong thing. I cannot understand why God chose to create a world with free will. After all, God must have known that we would misuse our free will and cause each other needless injury, pain, and death.

I wish God would offer us an explanation for creating a world with a seemingly endless capacity—and appetite—for cruelty.

But just because some people choose to misuse the capacity of free will hardly means that there is no God.

When God said, in effect, "I'm giving you free will," God wasn't kidding.

"In a perfect world," writes Eliezer Berkovits, "there would be no challenge and no choice, no decision and no responsibility. Perhaps, it would be some ideal form of reality, of which we cannot form the slightest notion. . . . It is not a universe of puppets. . . . No doubt, God took a risk with creation by granting it consciousness and free decision."[7]

A risk indeed. How could God permit the Holocaust, which my grandfather somehow escaped—unlike his parents and the rest of his family, all of whom perished under the Nazis? And then how could God permit murderers to slay him twenty-three years later?

And how could his grandson end up writing a book favoring the idea of close contact with God? What's that all about?

This is how I made my peace with God:

I do not hold God responsible for the actions people take.

No one knows why God created the human species with free will, and therefore with the possibility of causing both joy and tragedy. But just because the world is this way doesn't mean that there is no God. Or that God is automatically evil or cruel. God, in some sense, is like a parent who waits for his or her children to work things out with the other children. Why God doesn't intervene is a mystery. But can finite human beings realistically expect to understand an infinite being? No, not really.

And just because we don't fully understand something doesn't mean it doesn't exist. I don't understand the law of gravity yet I've never gone flying off into space. And neither have you.

If I were God, I probably would not have had the courage, or the faith in human nature, or whatever trait it took, to create a world where people were given free will.

In my world, people would be happy and healthy all the time. And there would be no suffering or death. But when God created the world, I wasn't consulted!

Is it possible to have a world where people can choose to do good things and to love one another if they do not have the choice to do the wrong thing as well?

God must have something in mind.

For those who went through the Holocaust and lost virtually everything, the question of "What could God be thinking?" becomes even harder. The most difficult thing in recent Jewish history to reconcile with the idea of a loving God is, of course, the Nazi Holocaust.

"Where was God?," we ask bitterly. Eliezer Berkovits, who addressed himself to this question in a profound and moving book, *Faith After the Holocaust*, asks a different question. Not where was God, but where was man?[8]

Once it was known that the Germans were killing Jews by the millions, Berkovits points out, it would have been easy to bomb the railroad tracks leading to the death camps. Well before then, it would have been easy for the United States and other countries to admit Jewish refugees fleeing the Nazi terror. But the American government so often refused.

We still have to wonder whether the creation of a world with the possibility of goodness and beauty makes sense, given the unavoidable accompaniment of the possibility of cruelty and destructiveness. Berkovits does not seem satisfied that a world with pretty sunsets justifies a world of pain and misery. He writes: "Yet all this does not exonerate God for all the suffering of the innocent in history."[9] I agree completely. It's God's world, and therefore it is God's responsibility. Again, though, just because I don't understand God does not mean that God doesn't exist, or doesn't care about the world or you and me.

Granted, we do not have the explanation *right now*. But must we conclude, therefore, that God does not exist?

The prophet Isaiah quotes God as saying that "My thoughts are not like your thoughts."[10] In other words, don't even bother trying to understand God's infinite thinking with your finite mind. The Jewish model of God accepts the idea that God is at one and the same time a trusted friend and a distant monarch, close and far, accessible and hidden. God seems possible when we admire a starry night or a field of wildflowers. God seems least likely when we hear about a family killed in a fire set by an arsonist. But either God is or God isn't; and either God is ultimately responsible for everything or God is responsible for nothing.

In sum, if the concept of good has no meaning, is nothing in a world without free choice, how could a loving, all-powerful God create a world without the *possibility* of evil?

I don't agree with those who say that evil is human nature. Evil is a *perversion* of human nature, which, despite everything I read in the newspapers or see on television, has enormous capacity for good. The fact that some people, or even many people, choose to take moral shortcuts in life does not have to make me a pessimist.

In sum, while God created a world in which bad things happen, I do not hold God responsible for the choices people make; and with my finite human mind I cannot figure out a way to create a world of love and beauty without giving people free will. And with free will comes the right to choose to do the wrong thing.

*

Today, we have an *expectation* of happiness, the right to the pursuit of which is written into the American Declaration of Independence. We expect not only happiness in life but satisfaction from our work, eternal love from our relationships, and perfectly healthy, loving, and respectful children. (Unless, of course, they're teenagers.)

At no time in human history have *expectations* about life been so impossibly high.

We have these expectations because improvements in medicine, communications, travel, and technology have given us a frame of mind wherein we assume that everything is going to be just the way we want.

But when disaster strikes, we are often *spiritually unprepared* for it. Our high expectations have programmed us to think that bad things will never happen—or will never happen to us.

In eras gone by, prior to the inflation of expectations, people did not feel this way about life. They did not expect that every child born would be healthy, or would even survive the first year. They did not expect their lives to be free of crisis or disaster. While they might not have seen their existence as taking place in the proverbial "vale of tears," they certainly did not assume that their lives would run perfectly smoothly.

And yet they believed in the existence of God; and they believed that God was loving and merciful and just. How could this be? Earlier generations of Jews suffered considerably for being Jewish. How could they reconcile their experience of personal and communal tragedy with the idea of a compassionate God?

The answer the authors of the Talmud provided eighteen hundred years ago is surprising to modern ears. The talmudists believed that suffering was a form of purification. We're *all* imperfect, we all do the wrong thing sometimes, and so we experience suffering as a way to purify ourselves.

Why do good people suffer, or suffer in ways disproportionate to whatever minor sins they may have done? How could innocent children die of disease or at a murderer's hands? The authors of the Talmud explained that when the general moral climate of a society is poor, then everyone suffers tragedy and loss, regardless of how well they live their lives. This argument certainly applies to our world today, where the moral climate keeps slipping and the level of indiscriminate suffering keeps rising. Nothing about today's world would have surprised the rabbis who compiled the Talmud.

When the moral climate is poor, says the Talmud, everyone suffers. Good people find themselves in the wrong place at the wrong time. People lose their health, or their lives, seemingly at random. And when you look at the big picture, we live in a world that places an extremely low value on morality—in terms of culture, government, and personal behavior. Madonna didn't get rich singing, "We're living in a spiritual world, and I am a spiritual girl," did she?

In short, decent people may suffer now, the talmudists believed, but their suffering will purify them and guarantee that they receive a reward in the afterlife.

Afterlife? Do Jews really believe in an afterlife? Absolutely.

For three thousand years, Jews have held to the idea that something awaits us when this life is over. The exact nature of that "something" eludes us. Our prophets, our rabbis, and our mystics have all come up with different possibilities, which we will consider later on. But the essential idea of Judaism is that this world is not all there is.

The nineteenth-century reformers removed from Judaism the idea that there might be an afterlife where the good are rewarded for living good lives. The idea of a hereafter, however, had existed in Judaism almost from its earliest days. We modern Jews tend to equate any idea of afterlife with Christian concepts of angels with harps and halos, devils with pitchforks, and fire and brimstone. Jews traditionally believed that people who led good lives were rewarded and that people who didn't weren't. The belief that something better awaited them down the road made it possible to accept the idea that decent people could suffer in this lifetime.

Orthodox Jews in today's world still believe that there is a world-to-come infinitely more blissful than this one, a world without hate or violence or death. Most American Jews are usually quite surprised to hear that Judaism has always maintained that the soul will outlive the body. Ironically, these ideas are becoming palatable to many Jews today, through exposure to Christian, Buddhist, and New Age sources. The last place most modern, educated Jews would think to look for a belief system involving any sort of life after death is in Judaism.

The belief in an afterlife with rewards and punishment made it possible for Jews who lived in eras prior to our own to accept that in this world, in this life, good people could suffer while evildoers enjoyed the fruits of their bad acts.

Those who live in immoral times—our own era, for example—sometimes suffer the fallout from the evil that others do. My grandfather was a decent person and an honest businessman. He had the misfortune to fall prey to a vicious criminal. The six million martyrs of the Holocaust were ordinary people who got caught in the maw of an extremely evil government and ideology. Do I blame God? Do I hold God responsible? Or do I say to myself, what can I do as a human being to increase the level of goodness in the world?

*

There is another reason why some people have trouble believing in God. All of us, at one time or another, have looked for God and prayed, and then have felt that God let us down. The classical example is the pony we asked for and never got for our birthday when we were children, but usually the matters about which we prayed were considerably more serious.

There are no atheists in foxholes, or, for that matter, in emergency rooms. Unaccustomed to prayer, we ask, we plead with God to keep someone alive, to let the car accident be something less than fatal, to guide the surgeon's hands, to give us one more day or week or birthday or anniversary in the company of someone we love.

We may try to cut a deal with God: "If You do this, I will . . . go to services, light candles, keep the Sabbath, pray more often, give charity, anything. God, you tell me what you want and I'll do it, if only you will come through for me this one time."

And if the results are contrary to what we pray for, we may feel that God has rejected our offer—and rejected us, as well.

Ten years ago, when I writing my first book about Judaism, a friend said, "Michael, you don't realize that Jews only think about God three days a year."

If someone we love, God forbid, is in a serious accident or is diagnosed with a fatal illness, the number of days during which we think about God leaps from three per annum to four.

Or if the state of crisis lingers, five.

We never feel good about another person who does not even respond to us when we reach out, especially if we are at a moment of crisis. What happens if, on the only occasions we reach out to God because we want to, even need to, and not because the Jewish calendar tells us to do so—we are left with our wishes unfulfilled, and worse, left with a feeling that our wishes weren't even heard or taken seriously?

How are we going to feel about God?

We are not going to feel especially close or hopeful. We will not come away from such a prayer experience with a renewed sense of God's nearness. Of course not. And God will be associated in our minds with the death of the loved one, with the surgeon leaving the operating theater with the sad expression that needs no words to explain, with the accident site, with the morgue.

Where was God when you cried out?

For many of us who in a time of need have sought a relationship with God, such an experience may well cause us to give up on the idea.

We need to remember that only once has a Jew ever seemed to have won a negotiation with God— Abraham, who skillfully manipulated God into promising not to destroy the city of Sodom if a certain number of righteous individuals could be found therein.[11] Abraham got God down from a hundred righteous people to a mere ten. Alas, God revealed a much stronger negotiating position when Abraham could not find even ten honest men in the city.

From that time on, there has never been an instance of a Jew successfully bargaining with God.

God apparently does not equate bargaining with prayer.

Prayer in the Jewish tradition does not mean telling God what we want, and making an offer of what we might do for God if we get our way.

After all, what exactly do we bring to the table? What can we do for God?

Prayer in Judaism means pouring out our heart to God, either through formal, fixed prayers or our own words and tears. Prayer in Judaism means a continuing conversation with God. We tell God our feelings; we cannot tell God what to do. God just doesn't seem to work that way. God, apparently, doesn't do deals.

And yet many of us base our anger at God or distance from God on an experience or series of experiences in which we prayed for a specific result, didn't get it, and felt that God didn't hear us, didn't care about us, or simply turned a deaf ear.

If we blame God for not doing things our way, if we blame God for seeming to ignore us when we most need help, if we allow unreal expectations about life to cut off our end of the conversation, whom are we hurting? God or ourselves?

*

Another thought to consider is that when we judge for ourselves what is good and what is bad or evil, what God should or should not do, sometimes we're just plain wrong.

A marriage ends in divorce. At the moment the parties feel guilt, shame, a sense of failure. Two years later (perhaps after some time with a therapist to understand why things didn't work out), the result may be a considerably happier marriage to someone else. A drunk-driving arrest and a humiliating night in jail may lead an alcoholic to sobriety. Being fired from a job may cause you to realize that you never wanted to go into that line of work in the first place. In short, we are not always the best possible judges of what is good and bad for us. Sometimes we blame God for something without understanding that the long-term results may actually be in our best interests.

*

Still another reason why it may be hard to accept the idea of God is that we are horrified by the things people do in God's name. We mentioned earlier the pathetic spectacle of televangelists offering salvation in exchange for your MasterCard number. Such behavior cheapens God in our eyes.

Far more damaging is the fact that millions of people who call themselves religious believe they have the right to kill in God's name. They belong to every religion and live in every corner of the globe. Terrorists in the Middle East; religious factions in the former Yugoslavia; a variety of minority ethnic groups in the former Soviet Union; Catholics and Protestants in Northern Ireland; Muslims and Hindus in India and Pakistan; American militia members; even some Jews— all believe they have the right to kill other people in the name of God.

Thinking people find this repulsive. They sense, rightly, that God is God, and that different religions simply represent different paths to the same Being. How sad, how tragic to watch God's children killing one another, each acting in the firm belief that this is what God wants.

The result: we unconsciously equate religion with fanaticism and disregard for the rights—and lives—of others. Many people wonder whether the world might not be better off without religion altogether. It certainly seems to cause far more harm, devastation, and tragedy than good.

And on a subconscious level, many blame God for letting the supposedly religious murderers get away with the killing—and, as well, with feeling that their acts are divinely justified.

If God really existed, they ask, why would all this be permitted?

Once again, the answer comes back to free will. God truly does not interfere when people choose to do the wrong thing, whether that wrong thing is as small as cutting off another driver on the highway or as large as giving the order for an attack that will kill thousands.

If we want to understand God on God's terms, we cannot really hold God responsible for the things that murderous fanatics do. In our minds, we need to detach God from those who justify doing evil in the belief that their deeds have been inspired by God.

*

Here's a surprising reason for doubt: Sometimes we have a hard time accepting the idea of God simply because we do not like authority figures.

In discussions about spirituality, people often describe their concept of God with words like *distant, angry, unhelpful, not there for me, doesn't want to see me succeed.* At those moments, I always think, "All right. Now tell me about your father."

Many Jewish prayers and religious texts speak of God as a father and a king; the gender of our millennial liturgy is, as we all know, unswervingly masculine. This fact alone makes it hard for many people to reconnect to traditional forms of Judaism. Those who have had a hard time, for one reason or another, with one or both of their parents often have a hard time with a God frequently described as a parent.

You no longer have to view God, consciously or unconsciously, as an invisible, all-powerful, larger version of either or both of your parents.

*

Let's examine one last impediment on the road to an understanding of God. Because the religious are so often belittled, we may wonder whether those of us who are intelligent and well educated (and let us assume, for the sake of argument, that we really are) can possibly believe that God exists. Well, Carl Jung based his approach to psychotherapy on spirituality. The Founding Fathers believed in God. The members of the Association of Orthodox Jewish Scientists all believe in God. Nowadays God sometimes seems to be the exclusive property of terrorists and televangelists. But lots of highly intelligent people believe in God; they're just a little quieter about it.

*

It takes a certain amount of courage to have faith in a world like this one. It takes special courage for Jews, who so recently underwent the Holocaust, to reach out to God. It's so hard for us because we are trained to think in secular terms, and we often come to a discussion of God with serious doubts.

If you can accept the idea that there is some explanation for the existence of hardship and suffering, even if we are not sure of what that explanation might be; if you can consider the notion that God hears prayers but rarely strikes deals; if you can stop blaming God for what human fanatics do in God's name, you are beginning to understand the traditional Jewish idea of who God really is. And the question "Who is God?" is the topic of the next chapter.

4

Clues

You will find in the Bible an account of the creation of the world, the formation of the Jewish people, the exodus from Egypt, the years in the desert, and the conquest of the land of Israel. You'll discover the first thousand years of the history of the Jewish people under the authority of God, prophets, and kings. You will find King Solomon building the First Temple in Jerusalem, and you will find Nebuchadnezzar destroying it as the prophet Jeremiah looked on and lamented. You will find love poetry and genealogies, battle songs and mourning customs, faith and faithlessness, cruelty and justice.

You will also find many clues to the nature of God, for Jews have always understood Jewish history as the history of the relationship between the Jewish people and God.

The most striking characteristic of the Bible for many readers is that it may be the sacred history of the Jewish people, but they do not figure at all in the first part of the story it recounts. And when they do show up, they are hardly heroic as individuals. Moses, a stutterer, had a wicked temper. Jacob tricked his father—with his mother's connivance. Judah went to a prostitute. Joshua sent spies to cut a deal with a prostitute in the town of Jericho. Joseph's vindictiveness nearly shattered his father's heart. Miriam gossiped about her brother Moses. Sarah laughed at her husband's idea of faith.

I find the Bible credible precisely because it does not talk about a super-race of spiritual beings who obeyed God's every word. The Bible describes people who sound a lot like people today. Times were different but human nature wasn't. People struggled emotionally and spiritually. The Bible is the record of the answers they found.

Those who have not spent much time dipping into the Bible may think of it as a book one turns to in moments of great spiritual torment. (Why else would the Gideons, the association of Christian business and professional men and women, put a copy in every hotel room, unless they were simply trying to inflict guilt on would-be adulterers?)

We expect that we can open the Bible to any page and find words of comfort and healing, soothing words that will reorient us toward a sense of inner peace. But that's not the Bible, that's Kahlil Gibran.[12]

The Bible can be absolutely mystifying to anyone encountering its pages for the first time. It jumps, like an oddly spliced movie, from genealogies to religious wars, from sexual and dietary restrictions to soulful prophecies.

Now, we view the Bible from our post-Freudian stance as a poorly organized collection of myths. We don't see it as a work of history. For thousands of years, though, Jews considered the Bible a book of history—a living history, a textbook on God. Taken as a textbook, what does the Bible tell us about the God who spoke to Abraham, to Moses, to all the Jews at Mount Sinai? Who is the God of the Bible?

In the beginning, we're told, God created the heaven and the earth. This raises the question of where God came from. The Bible doesn't even try to answer that one. Indeed, the Talmud dissuades us from asking what is above the universe or below it, or how God came into existence, or what happens after the universe runs its course. Judaism has always been a practical religion; these questions, however fascinating, have no practical application. We wouldn't live our lives differently if we knew how God came into being or what will happen in a few billion years if and when the universe ever runs its course; the Talmud basically tells us not to worry about it.

The Bible begins with God creating the universe. Unlike other ancient religious works, the Bible offers no genealogy of God—no divine parents, no childhood, no rivals, no lovers. No Mount Olympus teeming with jealous gods and rivalries. No family album. From the beginning, God is God—alone, dignified, creative, giving.

Sometimes people assault the authenticity of the Bible by pointing out that similar stories occur in other cultures; they argue that the Bible's validity as a religious document is compromised by the many signs of cross-cultural borrowing.

It is absolutely true that other religions of the time had creation stories not unlike ours; stories of a great flood appear in the writings of faiths other than Judaism. But that's not the point. David J. Wolpe, lecturer in modern Jewish thought at the University of Judaism in Los Angeles, explains it this way:

"Many find it hard to believe the Torah is divine when it contains stories or ideas identical to those of other, contemporaneous civilizations. . . . God was communicating in terms that would be understood by ancient Israelites. They knew certain ideas and terms, so God simply took those ideas, changed them, added to them, and refined them."[13]

Historian Yehezkel Kaufmann writes that the Bible

borrows ideas about the creation of the world from Babylonian writings. Yet, he points out, it does not place the creation of the Jewish people at the beginning of time. A reader must plow on for forty-eight chapters before the name Israel even comes up; and even then there is no indication that the Bible is a history of the Jewish people or its relationship with God.[14] I find this humility appealing.

If the Bible, then, is a history book, or a textbook on God, the next question is obvious: who wrote it?

Traditional Judaism tells us that God dictated the books of Genesis, Exodus, Numbers, Leviticus, and all but the last eight verses of Deuteronomy to Moses. Those last verses contain the facts of the death and burial of Moses. There are two traditions explaining the authorship of these lines. According to one, God dictated them to Moses, whose eyes filled with tears as he wrote them down; according to the other, God gave the lines to Joshua, Moses' successor.

Until late in the nineteenth century, most Jews believed the Bible to be of divine origin. That moment in history witnessed a growth in influence of the views of a German scholar named Julius Wellhausen, who sought to prove that the Bible—more specifically, the Pentateuch—was the work of several anonymous authors whose individual contributions could be identified by analysis of literary style and choice of vocabulary. Passages in the Bible in which God is referred to as

Jehovah were the work of one author. Those in which God was called Elohim were by a different person altogether. Passages that contained laws about how the priests should conduct themselves were by a third.

According to Wellhausen, these three bodies of writing, known as the J source (for Jehovah), the E source (for Elohim), and the P source (for Priestly), were combined with the Book of Deuteronomy (the D source) to produce the first five books of the Bible, known variously as the Pentateuch, the Torah, and the Five Books of Moses.

Although it is still taught as historical truth in most colleges, Wellhausen's theory has lost favor among many contemporary biblical scholars. For one thing, many ancient Near Eastern gods had more than one name, not just the Jewish God. Moreover, there is *no evidence* that the amalgamation of texts he postulated ever took place. Beyond that, there is the question of what "authenticity" means in this context. Certainly a book which has inspired most of the human race must by definition be a significant religious document.

Despite all this, however, I should mention that at least according to one Orthodox Jewish scholar, Rabbi Mordecai Breuer, none of the findings of the Higher Criticism—the analytical study of the Bible in accord with modern critical methods—precludes the belief that the Bible is of divine origin. In other words, even if there *had been* a cutting-and-pasting of source material into one Bible, God can still be the Author.

As we discussed above, some Jews believe that the Bible was divinely inspired—that God essentially dictated it to one or two people. Others consider it holy because Jews have considered it holy for thousands of years. Either way, the first time we find the Jewish people offered a special relationship with God comes when God reaches out to Abraham, in a puzzling series of events culminating in the near sacrifice of Abraham's beloved son Isaac.

This is one of the best-known and most difficult stories in the entire Hebrew Bible. How are we to make sense of it?

The first thing to note is that Abraham was not looking for God. God was looking for Abraham. God began the conversation. Abraham Joshua Heschel, the great Jewish theologian, describes it as "God's search for man, not man's quest for God."[15] Judaism was not founded by *mystics*, individuals possessed of an ability to reach up to God, to initiate contact with God, to start the conversation. Instead, Judaism began with a moment of *prophecy*, when a man suddenly realized that God was trying to talk to him.

The difference is huge. Abraham, you might say, didn't ask for the job of founding a people. The Bible records that he was wealthy and enjoyed a stable, if childless, marriage and a reputation for hospitality. He must have had massive, untapped resources of faith, for when it become apparent that God was speaking to him, promising him a son even though he was ninety-nine and his wife was ninety, he believed it.

Why did God reach out to a human being? What could God possibly need from us?

God "needs" nothing. But this one simple act of God's, reaching out to a mortal, finite human being—an old man, at that—tells us something critically important about Judaism. From God's first conversation with Abraham onward, Jews have understood themselves to be partners in a relationship with God. The purpose of the partnership is to complete the act of creation that God began in the first six 'days' of the universe.[16] How, one might ask, are we supposed to do this?

Our job is to increase the level of goodness in the world and assist God in completing the task of creation. Our purpose, then, is to be good and to do good, to develop our connection to God through thought and deed, to improve the world. This is why Jews, religious and secular, have been at the forefront of every major social change in modern times, from civil rights to psychology. Jews are imbued with a sense of communal responsibility that started when God first reached out to Abraham and said, in effect, "I want you to help me."

When God reached out to Abraham, Heschel writes, God "shattered man's illusion of being alone."[17]

Interestingly, Abraham did not respond with a request for proof of God's existence. He simply believed. Kaufmann writes, "It is one of the surprising features of the Bible that nowhere is the slightest attempt made to prove rationally that there is a God."[18] People in ancient times had no doubt that a god or gods existed. Faith came as standard equipment back then. They didn't need proof.

Judaism explains that *belief* in the existence of the One God, the God of Israel, is itself a *requirement* for Jews. If there were absolute, incontrovertible proof of the existence of God (whatever that might be; I don't think I could handle it), faith would hardly be a religious act. Faith would hardly take any courage.

At any rate, God broke the silence and reached out to Abraham, and made Abraham and Sarah and their household and their descendants—us—partners in the business of maintaining the world. God does God's part and expects us to do ours; this is the cornerstone of Jewish faith.

And then God did a very strange thing. God gave a couple in their tenth decade of life a son, and not long afterward asked Abraham to travel three days from home, build an altar and bind that son, and kill him as an offering to God.

In all probability, no other episode in the Bible is so troubling, and makes more readers doubt the fundamental decency and lovingkindness of God. I go back to my own experience as an adolescent in Sunday school in Roslyn, New York. None of us kids could figure that one out.

The classical Jewish commentators agree that God was testing Abraham; they debate whether Abraham *sensed* that God would relent at the last minute, as actually happened, and allow Abraham to substitute "a ram whose horns had caught in the brush."[19] I want to share my personal opinion with you. I have no doubt that Abraham knew all along that God would not make him go through with it.

Before I explain my reasoning, we should first ask how the idea of sacrifice found its way into the Bible. As with the creation and flood stories, there were certain religious concepts and practices that people in ancient times understood and regarded as normal. Sacrifice was the usual form of worship throughout the ancient Near East, and the Israelites might well have *rejected* a religion that did not include it. Asking them to do so might have offended or shocked them, and would certainly have amounted to a general too far out ahead of his troops. Again, David J. Wolpe: "After all, God could have dictated the U.S. Constitution [at Mount Sinai], but it would have done little good for ancient Israelites, for whom such notions would have been incomprehensible."[20]

God did prohibit human sacrifice. The Bible specifies an elaborate system of animal sacrifice, as well as meal and drink offerings, not because God needed them but because the Jews of that era needed them. Remember that the children of Israel were abandoning the worldview of the peoples around them, peoples who believed in many gods, and together with that, in fixed systems of signs and omens, mysterious oracles, magic, exorcism, and sorcery. Think about human nature. You simply cannot change everything at once.

Here now stands Abraham, the knife poised at his beloved son's throat. What are we to make of a God who put a lonely follower in such a horrible position? Why am I so certain that Abraham knew a happy ending was in store?

God was telling Abraham, "If you really want to follow me, if you really want to have me in your life, I have to come first. I have to come ahead of your love of your family. I have to come ahead of your desire to go down in history as the father of a great and numerous people. I have to be first, because when you keep me first in your life, everything else that you want and need will fall into place. Am I or am I not number one?"

Put yourself in Abraham's position. You have had a child very late in life, and you have expectations, aroused by a promise from God, that through this child you will be the father of a great people. All of your hopes and dreams center on the survival of this child. What clearer indication could you give that you are going to make God the first priority in your life, even at the seeming cost of all that you value?

Of course Abraham knew what God was asking. If Abraham was able to hear the voice of God, to recognize that God had chosen him for some greater purpose, then Abraham was wise enough to recognize the purpose behind this test. There was no doubt in Abraham's mind that he would return safely. The text of Genesis supports this interpretation.

Abraham and Isaac did not go off alone; two young servant boys accompanied them, along with a donkey for their belongings, according to Genesis 22:3. On the third morning, when they reached the point from which they could see the place for the altar far off in the distance, Abraham told the servants, "You stay here with the donkey; the lad [Isaac] and I will go alone and pray, and we will return to you then."

We. Not *I.* Abraham knew.

The message for us as Jews living more than three thousand years after the time of Abraham is this: Are we willing to put God first? Could we put God ahead of everything in our lives—our hopes, our dreams? What priority is God for us?

Today, we're taught to think of the Bible as a book of stories, a collection of laws, legends, and myths. For all but the last hundred and fifty years of Jewish history, however, Jews considered the Bible the blueprint of the universe and of their own lives. Today we want to know whether the events in the Bible happened as described.

Was there an Abraham? Did God speak to him and command him to sacrifice Isaac?

Of course we have no way to answer this question. A better question is this: why is this perplexing event recorded in the Book of Genesis?

One might argue that the story depicts a cruel and irrational God who comes to only a moment before it is too late. One might also argue that this story is proof of the Bible's irrelevance to modern life. We ourselves would never put a story about a father forced to slaughter his son in a religious book.

And yet. Heschel again: The Bible is "not a book composed for one age, and its significance cannot be assessed by the particular moral and literary standards of one generation. Passages that were considered outdated by one generation have been a fountain of comfort to the next."[21]

If you were writing the Bible, how would you choose a single event that would speak to individual Jews thousands of years into the future? What image would you offer that would resonate as much for readers in the far distant future as for readers in your own generation?

The binding of Isaac is as powerful a story now as it was then. When you think about how movies even fifteen or twenty years old can look dated or stale, you begin to get a sense of the unique power of the Bible to last thousands of years and yet still remain fresh in the mind's eye of the reader. The idea of a father's willingness to sacrifice his son is the vehicle the Bible chose in order to illustrate the importance that God was meant to play in the lives of people of all eras.

What can we deduce about the Jewish conception of God from this event? We see that God is not just a "911 God," or a God of the emergency room. The Jewish God clearly wants our attention more than three days a year. Sometimes we hear people say, "I don't really like religion because it's just a crutch. I think it's for weak people."

Judaism has never existed merely to serve people or make people's lives easier. Granted, many of the beliefs and traditions give life meaning and depth. But Judaism is not a feel-good religion. Judaism, a lot of the time, is a nuisance. Its requirements, at whatever level one observes them, can feel burdensome. No bread for the week of Passover. No food on Yom Kippur. Sabbaths and holidays intruding on the work and school calendar. For Sabbath observers, no driving, no television, no movies, no ball games, from sundown Friday until sundown Saturday. For those who consider it important only to marry within the faith, serious limitations on one's choice of partner. The more one gets involved, the more work it takes.

Again, Heschel: "Abraham was not going to sacrifice his only son in order to satisfy a personal need, nor did Moses accept the [Ten Commandments] for the sake of attaining happiness."[22] While you may feel good about being Jewish or about expressing your Jewishness in one way or another, Judaism was never and is not now about the pursuit of happiness. It's about a people called to serve God. That's how it was three thousand years ago. In all that time, that aspect of Judaism—the idea of keeping God first—never changed.

When I was a first-year law student, my contracts professor gave each of us a letter in which he remarked, that we hear a lot about students' rights but very little about students' responsibilities. You could apply the same idea to Judaism. With Judaism, the question is not "What's in it for me? The questions are "What's my responsibility? What can I do for someone else?" This kind of relationship with God demands sacrifice. Perhaps not as great as the sacrifice God initially asks of Abraham. The Jewish God is unquestionably giving and loving. But our God is *demanding*, too.

The Jewish concept of God, therefore, is that of a dignified, creative Being—but one who expects a lot from us. No wonder, from the time of the golden calf to our day, we have spent so much time running away! What were we running from? What does God have in mind for us? That's what we'll discuss next.

5

The "Big Bang" Theory of Judaism

The binding of Isaac indicates the level of spiritual commitment that God wanted from Abraham. The revelation at Mount Sinai shows all Jews what God expects from them.

Never before or since in the history of religion has a religion made this claim. An entire nation—as many as two million people—witnessed a revelation from God. Islam began when Muhammad went alone into the desert and had a vision. Only a small number of individuals witnessed the acts of Jesus. Buddha was alone when his visions began. It took the followers of these individuals decades or centuries to create religions around events that had few or no eyewitnesses.

Sinai stands alone. Two million witnesses. And no minority reports—no contemporaneous conflicting accounts. No one said, "I was there and it was nothing like what it says in Exodus!"[23]

The Bible and the Talmud tell us that before the two million children of Israel actually heard the voice of God at Mount Sinai, they underwent a terrifying experience of massive thunder and lightning, with the mountain itself literally lifting off the ground and being held over their heads.[24] From that moment on, the Jewish people existed as a people because of their collective belief that God had spoken to them, called them, chosen them, as a group. Writes Kaufmann, "The Jewish encounter with God determined the entire course of Jewish history. Because of it, Israel never surrendered to other religions or civilizations."[25]

The reason we are Jews today is that about thirty-two hundred years ago, *something happened*, and from that moment to this, Jews have thought of themselves as Jews. You can think of it as the "big bang" theory of Judaism. Just as we do not know from a scientific point of view precisely what happened at the beginning of the universe, we may not precisely know what happened at Mount Sinai. You may believe the biblical account or not. But clearly something happened, some massive explosion of consciousness, an entire people having a spiritual awakening.

No other religion on earth makes a similar claim. Christians and Muslims accept the idea that God spoke to the Jewish people at Mount Sinai; typically, Jews are the only ones skeptical of an event that much of the world's population has always accepted as a historical fact.

Skeptics tell us that much of what God told the Jewish people, such as the commands against theft and murder, existed in previous legal codes like that of the Babylonian lawgiver Hammurabi. This entirely misses the point about the importance of Sinai. *Here's the difference: Hammurabi was a human being who made laws. Sinai was the first time that God declared laws.* For the first time in history, people had a code of conduct based on an absolute—the word of God.

At Sinai, God gave the Jews—and through the Jews the entire world—a system of values, a sense of right and wrong, a concept of morality.

So it's no wonder the rest of the world couldn't stand us! Who wants to be reminded of morality?

And yet. Since Sinai, Jews have symbolized the idea that God has expectations for the behavior of every person. Many people do not want to be reminded of this fact; Jews throughout history have paid a high price for their belief in God's decision to use them as a vehicle to educate the rest of the world about morality. Indeed, the rabbis of the Talmud sadly noted the connection between the Hebrew word for Mount Sinai, pronounced *see-nye*, and the Hebrew word for hatred, *see-naw*.

You might say that today Jews are as moral or immoral as everyone else. That may be true, but it does not change the historical mission of the Jewish people, which was set forth at Mount Sinai: to live up to a moral standard determined not by people but by God. A Yiddish expression says, *es is shver tzu zein a yid,* "it's hard to be a Jew." It's not hard to see *why*, given the burden God placed on us Jews at Mount Sinai. And, according to tradition, every Jew, including you and me, stood at Sinai; like it or not, we are part of that great tradition.

Of course, it did not take the Jews two months after witnessing God at Mount Sinai to begin to run from the heavy responsibilities that had been placed upon them. When they thought Moses was just *one day late* coming back down the mountain after going up to get the Ten Commandments, they panicked, melted down their gold, created the golden calf, and worshipped it.

For me, this act of rebellion serves as one more reason to accept the divine origin of the Bible. If you believe that editors merged one source with another, cut and pasted, and came up with a finished document of some sort, you have to wonder why they failed to edit out all the parts of the Bible that present the Jewish people in a harsh light.

If they had done that, the Bible might be about as long as a pamphlet.

The Jews almost invariably rebelled against God and against their election by God to bring divine morality to the world. They had never asked for the job, and they cried repeatedly in the desert, even within weeks and months of Sinai, "Would that we had died back in Egypt!" They rebelled, they backslid, they worshipped the golden calf. Today archaeologists digging in Israel frequently make the embarrassing discovery of little idols in the houses of ancient Jews. Oops.

Even our leaders did not want their jobs, which seems hard to believe given today's world, where Jewish communal leaders seem never to meet a title they don't like. Moses, a self-conscious man with a terrible stammer, tried to persuade God to use someone else. Of the twelve advance agents whom Moses deputized to spy out the land of Israel and convince the Jews in the desert that everything would be fine—ten lied. They said that the land was full of unconquerable giants and we were better off in the desert. It's not surprising that Moses had a terrible temper. The list grows:

Jonah, when commanded to speak a prophecy to the city of Nineveh, promptly boarded a boat heading in the opposite direction. A rabbinical commentary in the Midrash suggests that he paid the fare for the whole ship so that it would leave immediately. Whether he paid one fare or chartered the vessel, he clearly sought to avoid God's command. Not very heroic behavior. Why didn't the "editors" edit that out?

Once the Jews entered the land of Israel, they immersed themselves in deceitfulness and backstabbing, all of which is recorded in painful detail in the Bible. So abhorrent was their behavior that God carried through on a repeated warning and, according to Jewish belief, sent Nebuchadnezzar, the king of Babylon, against them. The Babylonians destroyed Solomon's Temple in Jerusalem and forced the Jews into exile.

Jews have rebelled from the start against the role they did not ask to play—bearer of morality to an amoral world. It's not surprising that we still don't like the job. It's not surprising that we are frequently ambivalent about our own Jewishness. It's a source of pride, but it also can be a burden.

The 'main event' in Israel's history, as Heschel puts it, was God's giving of the Ten Commandments to Moses and the Jewish people at Mount Sinai. By that moment, as we all know from our Haggadahs, the "script" we follow at the Passover Seder table, Moses had led the children of Israel out of slavery in Egypt and brought them into the desert.

Why the desert? You can think of it as a spiritual training camp, a chance for a people, freshly and miraculously emerged from bondage, to be by itself, apart from the influences of other faiths, preparing for its mission to demonstrate godliness and be a sign of the One God from its home base in the land of Israel.

The Jews might not have understood *why* they had been selected, but they certainly had a clear idea of the God who had chosen them. The Bible offers a variety of clues to the character of God, and we can see just how different the biblical God was from any god or gods the ancient world knew.

First, the worship of God and communication with God included no intoxicants and no drugs. In contrast, the ancient Greeks, for example, believed that their gods took part in frenzied drunken celebrations and could even choose to have sex with the participants.

Second, the Jewish God spoke clearly and directly to people, either to everyone, as at Sinai, or to individuals, as with Abraham, Moses, or the other prophets. A prophet, Heschel writes, is someone who has a solid understanding of God and not just a guess as to what God might be about. Heschel expresses it as the difference between knowing about the idea of friendship and actually having a friend.[26]

Third, the Jewish God had no secret system of signs and omens that only an elite could understand. The Jewish people was from the beginning "a kingdom of priests";[27] anyone and everyone who wanted direct access to God could have it. In the Bible, people asked God about specific situations, such as loss of property, a painful pregnancy, sickness, and accidents, according to Kaufmann.[28] And God would answer directly or in dreams.

So far as the Israelites in the desert knew, Moses was the only recipient of divine revelation. But what happened when Joshua, one of his assistants, came running to him with the news that several individuals were prophesying in the desert camp? Another religion might have condemned this as a power grab. Moses' reaction: "I wish everybody was a prophet."[29] An innovation of Judaism was that anyone who wished a close relationship with God could have one. Pagan gods had selfish needs; the God of Israel did not.

Fourth, the Jewish God condemned magic, a staple of ancient religion. Magic gave human beings the power to be like gods. God's position was clear: God was God and you weren't. You could have a personal relationship with the Jewish God, but you could not usurp any of God's power through magic, exorcism, or any other means.

Finally, Jewish kings could not claim divine origins or divine powers. The Bible makes clear that they were often extremely fallible human beings. Throughout the later sections of the Bible, their failings are expressed in brutally honest terms. There were severe limits on the power of the kings of ancient Israel, and even on the number of horses they could own, lest their egos swell too large. The most significant limitation on their power was the absolute denial of their divinity. They were not gods and were not descended from God. Historian Kaufmann expresses it best:

> "In sum, then, the biblical religious idea . . . is of a supernal God, above every cosmic law, fate, and

compulsion, unborn, unbegetting; knowing no desire, independent of matter and its forces; a God who does not fight other divinities or powers of immunity; who does not sacrifice, divine, prophesy or practice sorcery; who does not sin and needs no expiation; a God who does not celebrate festivals of His life. An unfettered divine will transcending all being— this is the mark of biblical religion and that which sets it apart from all the religions of the earth."[30]

This was the God of the Bible, the God of Abraham, the God who spoke to two million Jewish men and women at Mount Sinai. While the world may have changed in the three thousand or more years since Sinai, God hasn't.

6

Stairways to Heaven

We've seen that the God of the Bible is a straightforward God, one whose manner of speech, expectations for behavior, firmness, and lovingkindness were easy to behold, if hard to live up to. This God was different from all the gods of the time because of a quality of aloneness.

And yet God was available to anyone who wished to know God better, to "hear" God's "voice." According to rabbinic teaching, more than a million Jews of the biblical era were prophets[31]—individuals so attuned to the idea of God that God spoke directly to them. In only a minuscule percentage of cases were the prophecies of those who heard from God recorded and included in the Bible.

Prophecy, the idea that God speaks to human beings who are able to hear God's voice, was a common feature of Jewish history in its first thousand years.

Unfortunately, as I mentioned before, so was backsliding.

Jews, we have seen, were never comfortable with their role of "light unto the nations,"[32] a people charged with symbolizing the existence of the one God. We ran from our responsibilities every chance we got, from the moment of the golden calf onward. Jews believed, though, that even though we might abandon God, God would never abandon us. From the time of destruction of the First Temple in 586 B.C.E., we believed that when the community as a whole suffered punishment, it was because the community as a whole *deserved* it. We have always taken responsibility for our actions.

When we ran from God's expectations, other peoples came and ravaged Jerusalem, destroyed our Temples, heaved us into exile, and perpetrated murderous acts against us. Yet we always saw the hand of God directing those other nations. If calamity befell the Jewish people, the Jewish people did not blame cruel fate or bad luck. We blamed our own behavior. We took responsibility for our actions—and for the consequences of those actions.

Here's an incredibly short version of Jewish history after Sinai:

We entered the land of Israel, at the direction of God and under the authority of Moses' successor, Joshua. We lived there under the authority of a succession of prophets, judges, and kings. Some of the kings were pious; others were idolatrous. Some, like David and Solomon, were poets or builders. David is credited with having written the Psalms. Solomon, tradition has it, wrote the Song of Songs as a lusty young man, the Book of Proverbs as a worldly-wise man of middle age, and Ecclesiastes ("There is nothing new under the sun") as a world-weary elder statesman. In between, he oversaw the construction of the great First Temple, Judaism's central house of worship, in Jerusalem.

Jews lived in the land of Israel in a steadily worsening moral climate marked, according to the Talmud, by three major sins: the practice of idolatry, engaging in improper sexual relationships, and vast bloodshed. When the Babylonians, under Nebuchadnezzar, lay siege to Jerusalem in the year 586 B.C.E., Jews began to realize that it was divine retribution for centuries of doing the wrong thing. God, they believed, could be patient for generations, but at some point one could no longer literally get away with murder. And so, acting through the conquering Babylonians, God exiled the Jews.

The theme of exile and redemption is a constant as Jewish history progresses. In 539 BCE the Persians took over; sometime later we created a new holiday, Purim, celebrating a new victory—avoiding genocide.

Fifty-two years after Nebuchadnezzar destroyed Jerusalem, the exiles returned to Israel from Babylon and built the Second Temple on the site of the first one.

Over the next six hundred years, Jewish life continued in the Promised Land. The Persians conquered Babylon, Alexander the Great conquered the Persians, and the Ptolemy and Seleucid dynasties, descended from his generals, divided his empire between themselves. Under one of the Seleucids, Antiochus IV, the Jews rebelled, and, under the Hasmoneans, eventually achieved independence and Jews gained a new holiday, Hannukah. This independence was short-lived—Rome was on its way to conquering the Mediterranean Basin.

Finally, however, unworthy behavior brought down another destroyer, this time the Romans. In the year 66 C.E., the inhabitants of Judea and Galilee rose up in revolt against Rome. The following year Vespasian's legions invaded the land of Israel and besieged Jerusalem; in the year 70 C.E. Jerusalem fell and the Second Temple was destroyed. Again the Jewish people went into exile, a state of communal homelessness, from which the first glimmer of redemption came nineteen hundred years later, with the founding of the modern State of Israel.

Why, incidentally, was the Second Temple destroyed? Why did God, in effect, unleash Rome to conquer Israel? This time, according to the sages, there were no three unpardonable sins but only one. The reason the Second Temple had been leveled (with the exception of one retaining wall, variously referred to as the Western or Wailing Wall) was that the Jews in the era of the revolt had been guilty of the crime of baseless hatred. And the only cure for baseless hatred, according to the nineteenth-century Jewish philosopher Rabbi Nachman of Bratslav, was a heavy dose of senseless love.

After the destruction of the Second Temple, some Jews remained in what was then called Palestine. Others left for Babylonia, the Tigris-Euphrates plain stretching from Baghdad to the Persian Gulf, where there had been a substantial Jewish presence since the sixth century B.C.E., or for one or another of the Jewish communities in the extensive diaspora around the Mediterranean basin.

Their descendants spread over the globe, throughout the countries of the Middle East, Europe, India, North Africa, and what is now Russia. In order to maintain some sense of connectedness and spiritual discipline, the leaders of the Palestinian and Babylonian communities organized and eventually wrote down the laws and traditions of the Jewish people. Their efforts over the next five centuries resulted in the two Talmuds, the Babylonian Talmud and the smaller, so-called "Jerusalem" Talmud, the ultimate compendia of Jewish law and knowledge that traditional Jews study even today. The Babylonian Talmud still directs the lives and modes of thought of observant Jews.

Although comprehensive and intellectually stimulating, the Talmud did not completely satisfy the need to approach God—even from the exile—in a way that transcended human thought. At some point along the way, some Jews came to believe they had also lost the ability to hear God's voice, to be prophets, to be attuned to a spiritual reality they could not see or touch. If God had stopped reaching out to the Jews, they concluded, then the Jews would have to begin reaching out to God.

We call the act of reaching out to God a "mystical" experience. The words *mystical* and *mysterious* come from the same Greek root, meaning "secret." One dictionary defines *mysticism* as "the doctrine that it is possible to achieve communion with God through contemplation and love without the medium of human reason."[33] Remember that the first exile lasted less than sixty years; now, centuries were piling up with no indication that God would ever let the Jews return home. Work began on the Zohar, a mystical commentary on the first five books of the Bible. The Zohar reinforced the sense Jews had that God was inside of them, that they possessed a divine soul, and that they could reach out to God, not simply by adhering to Jewish law, but through an awareness of the godliness within themselves.

Jewish thought, from that moment forward, developed in two distinct if complementary directions. One was the law, which could be found in the Talmud and related commentaries written in every century from those days to ours. Some talmudists began to explore this new, mystical approach to God. If God had ceased to speak to Jews, then Jews would have to find other ways to connect with their Creator, to relieve their sense of abandonment. Observing God's law as found in the Talmud and its commentaries was one approach. The mystical path was an exciting new way, supplementary to it. It appealed to increasingly large numbers of Jews.

The body of Jewish mystical tradition is known as the *Kabalah*, from a Hebrew root that conveys the idea of "receiving a tradition." Those who studied the mystical doctrines are called kabbalists. The insights about God and the universe with which they were occupied were regarded as secrets, and were often transmitted in private from one kabbalist to another.

The early kabbalists were interested in the beginning of creation; only later, as times got worse, did they turn their attention to "end of the world" questions. They wanted to know about the redemption of the soul in a world full of suffering.[34]

Among other things, the kabbalists reexamined the traditional forms of Jewish prayer and discovered that they encompassed a mystical way of looking at the human soul.

One easy way to get a taste of kabbalistic thinking is to look at the traditional morning prayer service. Now, the morning prayer service has barely changed over a thousand years. Jews who pray in the words of the traditional liturgy connect themselves to Jews all over the world who continue, even to the present day, to approach God in the same manner. They connect themselves, as well, to all the Jews over the last millennium who uttered the very same words every day of their lives. This awesome sense of connectedness is part of the overlooked power of traditional prayer, which, for much of Jewry, fell by the wayside as a result of the massive changes that took place in the early nineteenth century.

The kabbalists teach that the soul has five levels. *Nefesh* is the lowest level, and it is where the soul intersects with our physical selves. Next comes *ruach*, a wind blowing down from God's "mouth," as it were, to ours, a sort of divine CPR. The third level of the soul is *neshamah*, which is the "breath" of God, an act of intimacy between God and humankind. The highest level of the soul is *chayah*, the "life force," which, in the words of Aryeh Kaplan, an expert on Jewish spirituality, is "a realm that transforms thought . . . an awareness of the divine life force."[35] And then comes *yeœidah*, which means something like "unity" or "oneness." *Nefesh, ruach, neshamah, chayah, yechidah*: these, the kabbalists tell us, are the rungs of the ladder that connect our physical selves to our deepest spiritual longings. We will discuss the first four levels. Little is known about the fifth, *yechidah*. Certainly I know nothing about it. With that caveat in mind, let's go on.

Just as the soul has four aspects that can be understood and described, so does the morning prayer service, say the kabbalists. The first part of the service, the introductory readings and blessings, in which we express gratitude for our physical selves and the continuing miracle of our existence, corresponds to the level of *nefesh*, the interface of body and soul.

Next come the verses of praise, mostly culled from the Psalms, which express our gratitude to God for the greatness and beauty of the world around us and for our role as the chosen people. This second section of the morning prayers corresponds to the level of *ruach*, the wind from God, the awareness of the world that God created.

The third part of the service is the recitation of the central declaration of Jewish faith, the Shema, so named because it begins with the words *Shema yisrael adonai elohenu adonai echad*, "Listen, Israel. The Lord, our God—the Lord is One." Not three, not a hundred, but one. This prayer, taken from the Book of Deuteronomy, expresses the intimacy between the Jewish people and its God, an intimacy that was sealed with the revelation at Mount Sinai.

Traditionally, we close our eyes and cover them with our hand as we say the Shema, expressing the idea that regardless of what may be happening in the world around us, we still concentrate on that one idea, the idea of God's oneness. We are still on intimate terms with the one God, the God of the Bible, any time we choose to close our eyes to the physical world and transcend to a higher level. And this act of transcendence to an awareness of God and only God corresponds to the level of the soul called *neshamah*, in which we figuratively feel God so close to us that we even sense, as it were, God's breath.

The fourth key element of the morning service is the Amidah, so named from the Hebrew word meaning "standing." Since Talmudic times, Jews have risen to their feet when saying this nineteen-blessing prayer because of its great importance as the central core of the daily liturgy.

The Amidah incorporates all of the aspirations of the Jewish people. These include the desire for a close relationship with God, health, freedom, the rebuilding of the Temple in Jerusalem, an end to our state of exile, and the bringing of a redeemer. The kabbalists explain that it corresponds to the highest level of the soul, *chayah*, the life force. Putting our attention on our relationship to God transforms our thinking. Becoming aware of the divine, changes the way we live our lives.

The authors of the Zohar explained the four levels of the soul in other terms. In their explanation they used the metaphor of two lovers, the Jewish people and God. *Nefesh*, the interface of spiritual and physical, stood for the initial physical attraction between two persons. *Ruach*, the "wind" from God's mouth, symbolized the conversation between two persons attracted to one another. *Neshamah*, the "breath" of God, meant that moment when two persons are in such close physical proximity that they become conscious of each other's breath.

And *chayah*, awareness of the divine—the highest level of the soul—was the kiss.

Love, arousal, connectedness—such were the concepts of the early Kabbalists. But as time passed and conditions grew more perilous for the Jewish people, the concerns of the Kabbalists changed. In fact, the worse times were, the more the mystical route to God gained favor, and the more complex the mystical doctrines became.

Persecutions in England, Spain, France, and Germany from the ninth century through the fifteenth led to a sense of grave pessimism. If Mount Sinai had been the "Big Bang" of Jewish history, Jews now wanted a second, equally miraculous experience. Jews wanted a *redeemer*, a *Messiah*, a great spiritual leader. We yearned for an individual to suspend the laws of history and return us to a position of pride, honor, and safety. This desire has been a constant thread in Jewish history throughout the last thousand years.

The most influential of the Messianic kabbalists was a young man who lived in the middle of the sixteenth century, who wrote no books, and who died at the age of thirty-eight. His name was Isaac Luria. Fortunately for history, one of his students, Hayim Vital, wrote down Luria's ideas in a volume entitled *Etz chayim*, the "Tree of Life." Luria's ideas appealed to Jews on a spiritual level and, as we shall see, on a political level too.[36]

How did God create the world? It's complicated; stick with me. If God occupied all of the universe, a space for the world had to be vacated within God's own self. Luria used the Hebrew term *tzimtzum* to designate this withdrawal, or "shrinking." The result was an empty space surrounded by God. God then placed the divine element of *din*, or "judgment," into that empty space. God's capacity for judgment, of course, can be very destructive if unchecked, so God caused a thin line of divine light to enter the circle. The divine light is a beam of light but also, symbolically, a "person" called Adam Kadmon, or Original Man.

Good things radiated from the nose, ears, and mouth of this Adam Kadmon/divine light; a divine "crown," wisdom, and intelligence all entered the empty space, all helping to shape the newly developing world in beneficial ways, all tempering the initial attribute of divine judgment that God had placed in the empty space.

As these spiritual elements helped create the world, God prepared other traits, called *sefirot*, or "emanations," necessary for the Creation. The sefirot include mercy, patience, majesty, and compassion. Each radiated via "pure light" from God through Adam Kadmon's eyes and into that circle.

In order to protect the sefirot from intermingling, the pure light of each one was wrapped in a shell. The shell was actually a "thicker" form of light. Each divine emanation, therefore, was encompassed, as if in a glass tube, in a shell of thick pure light. These shells of thicker light are called *kelipot*. God poured the pure light of each sefirah—the mercy, patience, majesty, and compassion necessary for the creation of the world—into its separate *kelipah*, or shell, of thicker light. How did these beams of light enter the circle containing the formless void from which the world would be formed? Through the "eyes" of Adam Kadmon.

But then a catastrophe occurred. The *kelipot* shattered. This tragic moment is called *shevirat ha-kelim*, the Breaking of the Vessels. The pure light scattered. Some returned to God, but many of the divine sparks were trapped in the formless void. So there was chaos, nothing in its proper place. God stepped in, restoring order and actually creating the world, envisaging humanity as an assistant in the process of redeeming the divine sparks lost at the moment of the Breaking of the Vessels.

In the Garden of Eden, Adam's sin repeated the catastrophe of *shevirat ha-kelim*. The role of every Jew, Luria concluded, was to help restore the lost sparks to their divine source, thereby redeeming the world. This would be accomplished by observing God's law and praying.

Luria's complex imagery was embraced "eagerly," from "Persia to England, Germany to Poland, Italy to North Africa, Holland to Yemen[, giving] new hope in the midst of despair."[37]

Why were these ideas so appealing throughout the Jewish world? The idea of God sending a part of God into exile made sense to a people living in exile. Keep in mind that Luria was teaching in the 1560s, a time when the exile from Spain in 1492 was just about as recent and traumatic as the Holocaust is to us.

Jews everywhere, therefore, identified strongly with the idea that *we ourselves* were "divine sparks" who had been "scattered" when our own vessels—our communities in Spain and elsewhere—had been shattered. And it gave us new impetus to turn to prayer and good deeds.

Remember that Jews traditionally believed that our own misdeeds had caused the exile. Just as Adam, for his sin, had been driven from the Garden of Eden, so we were twice driven from our homeland—and we were still living in exile. Now we had the opportunity to redeem ourselves, to prove ourselves worthy of God's attention, love, and care once again. Lurianic kabbalism, in short, offered both an explanation of horrendous historical events and a basis for hope, suggesting that Jews, no matter how weak their political position, could always find their way, through prayer and action, back to God.

The kabbalism of Isaac Luria may not speak to the Jew today with the intensity and certainty that it did a few centuries ago, although it remains an object of fascination for many. Our current political and economic position is so strong that we do not really feel "exiled."

We do not easily think in esoteric terms like "shells of light" and "emanations of God." Conversely, the Jews of Luria's day, whose imagination was great enough to invent these concepts, could never have dreamed of the kind of freedom we Jews enjoy today.

Despite the changed political circumstances, and despite its complexity, kabbalism still fascinates many Jews. At least two factors explain this phenomenon. Number one: the sense Jews have that Kabbalah is ours; other groups may have other mystical approaches to God, but this one is authentically Jewish. And number two: it demonstrates that Jews still want to find a way to deepen their spirituality. We are heirs to an unbroken tradition of connectedness to the One God. The desire to be with that One God is an eternal flame burning in each of us. Kabbalah appeals because it is complex, mysterious, and authentically Jewish.

They say of Kabbalah that those who understand it do not talk about it, and those who talk about it do not understand it. With no false modesty, I place myself in the second category. The introduction I offer barely scratches the surface of Jewish mysticism. If the subject appeals to you, I urge you to seek out sources more knowledgeable about it than I am.

Just as the Talmud was a closed book to anyone lacking the time or education to learn its complicated ways, so too was Lurianic kabbalism inaccessible, because of its complexity, to the average unlettered Jew.

The problem arose: how to bring hope and meaning to the lives of Jews who had not been educated in either the legal or the mystical tradition?

Israel ben Eliezer, in the eighteenth century, was not a noted scholar. An extremely poor man, he lived in southern Poland's Carpathian Mountains. Around the age of thirty-six, he became a faith healer and exorcist. He traveled from village to village in the mountains, healing the sick. As he made his way, he developed a new form of Kabbalah, one that even uneducated Jews could savor.

The fall of those divine sparks, said Israel ben Eliezer, was not the disaster Luria claimed. Rather, the sparks "were lodged in every item of creation, and this meant that the whole world was filled with the presence of God. A devout Jew could experience God in the tiniest action of his daily life—while he was eating, drinking or making love to his wife—because the divine sparks were everywhere."[38]

Israel ben Eliezer, better known as the Baal Shem Tov, founded Hasidism. This movement gave Jews who could not afford to dedicate themselves entirely to the study of Talmud a stake in the Jewish religion. Today, many Chasidic movements have yeshivas of their own and combine intellectual study with spiritual and emotional attachment to God.

What does all this mean to us today? How does all this information and history help us, right now, to better understand the relationship between Jews and God?

For me, the main point is that as times got worse, as they faced expulsions, crusades, discrimination, or genocide, Jews remained loyal to God anyway. They viewed the calamaties they faced as temporary. They kept their faith that God would take care of them. They found new, mystical ways to contemplate the idea of God. They went through trial and crisis. But they never stopped believing.

We've seen that early kabbalism sought to understand how the world began. Kabbalists then turned their attention to the desperate political plight of the Jewish people. And we've seen that later exponents of kabbalism began to answer a different question, namely, how do we get out of this jam, this combination of exile and discrimination?

The solutions came in two basic forms. One solution would arrive in this life: a Messiah, an avenger, a messenger of God, to deliver us from the seemingly perpetual state of crisis and powerlessness that had befallen us. The other answer was that this life was not all there was; that something even better awaited us; that, as the saying goes, "death is the night between two days—the day of life on earth and the day of the eternal life in the world-to-come."

The twin concepts of Messiah and afterlife were nothing new in Judaism; both ideas dated back to Biblical times. But as life in this world grew increasingly precarious, the ideas that a leader would come and that a life beyond death awaited us became more and more important. Who would the Messiah be? When would the Messiah arrive, and what would happen? And what is the Jewish belief about the concept of afterlife? These complex and fascinating questions are at the heart of the next chapter.

7

"We'll Be Right Back...
After This"

When things were bleakest in medieval times, Judaism took extremely seriously an idea that, in one form or another, had been a part of the faith since biblical days—that an individual would come, a champion, a person who would inaugurate a new and better world.

Who that person would be, and what he would do, has never been firmly ironed out. But the worse the times got, the more Jews embraced the idea that one individual, anointed by God, would save the day.

The term Messiah derives from the Hebrew word *mashiach*, which simply means "anointed one." In biblical days, a priest or prophet poured anointing oil on the head of a king or other leader as part of his inaugural ceremony; analogously, the Mashiach, or Messiah, is a leader anointed by God.

Belief in the coming of the Messiah translates directly into belief in God, who, after all, is trusted to send the Messiah at the right time. But what will the Messiah do? When will he arrive? Will the Messiah make an imperfect world perfect? Or will he arrive only when the earth's inhabitants have already made the world perfect themselves?

The debate raged on in Judaism, which for twenty centuries has not had a central authority to define religious beliefs. Different eras produced different messianic concepts; the one constant throughout Jewish history has been the belief that one day, when the time is right, the Messiah will come.

The messianic ideal in Judaism dates all the way back to the earliest days of Jewish history, perhaps as far back as the age of the Patriarchs in the Book of Genesis.[39]

The prophet Isaiah, who witnessed the destruction of the First Temple in 586 B.C.E., was quite specific in his expectations of what the Messiah would do. A remnant of the Jewish people would return to the land of Israel, Isaiah prophesied, and the Messiah would lead them and create a kingdom of justice and righteousness. He would be a warrior and a protector, and the day of his coming would be a great and glorious day. With God's sanction and spirit, the Messiah would rule in Zion and make Israel a model of righteousness for the world.[40]

No Messiah came in those days. We are still waiting.

Incidentally, this is what I didn't know to tell the kids from Kansas back when I was a teenager. Why don't Jews believe that Jesus is the Messiah? Because the Hebrew Bible is specific about the changes in the world that the Messiah would bring about. If those changes didn't occur, then the person isn't the Messiah. Christians sometimes point to certain verses in the Book of Isaiah and elsewhere in the Hebrew Bible and refer to these verses as "prooftexts" that predict that Jesus would be the Messiah. But if you read those texts, Jews believe, there's no real "proof" in them that they refer to Jesus.

One thing I've always admired about Judaism is that we've never claimed to have a hammerlock on the truth. The Jewish attitude toward other religions is not that they're wrong and we're right. It's that everyone is entitled to his or her beliefs. We don't try to convert anyone—if anything, Jewish law actually *requires* that we *dissuade* potential converts to Judaism. (We ask them, in effect, "Don't you have enough problems already without being Jewish, too?") And similarly, we respect the right of other people to believe what they want, and we ask that they respect our right to live by our beliefs.

That's a long way of saying that Judaism has no problem with Christians believing that Jesus is the Messiah; we just don't share that belief.

Because we talk so little in Sunday School about the concepts of Messiah and afterlife, many Jews, myself included, are quite surprised when they discover that a key tenet of Judaism, going back thousands of years, is the idea of the resurrection of the dead. As the prophet Daniel wrote, "Many that sleep in the dust will awake, some to everlasting life."[41]

Life after death, along with judgment for one's actions on earth, are vitally important parts of Judaism. We've always believed in the existence of a "heaven," where the soul dwells close to God; I'm very happy to report that we don't have any concept of an eternal, punishment-filled Hell.

In the Biblical conception of afterlife, God ruled a place called Sheol, where souls went after death to lead a shadowy existence; the Bible did not specify about what happened there. What went on in Sheol? We turn to some fascinating passages from Kaufmann for the answer:

> "The spirit of the deceased descends beneath the earth to Sheol, 'the pit,' the world of the shades, where it joins its departed ancestors and kin. Although kings sit there on their thrones, there is equality in Sheol; small and great, king and captive, master and slave sleep together. It is a land of deep darkness, a land of no return.

"Alongside this conception is another that links the soul with the grave and the interred body. Rachel weeps for her children in her sepulcher at Ramah. Necromancers spend the night in graveyards. Care of the corpse is crucial for the fate of its ghost. . . .

". . . To ancient man a name was a substantial matter; keeping up its memory after death gave vitality to the soul in the other realm. The deceased who is buried among his people and whose name is kept alive among them still shares, as it were, in life upon the earth."[42]

Further evidence of the biblical vintage of the belief that the soul lives on after the person dies comes from Judah Halevi's eleventh-century work, *The Kuzari*, which we discussed earlier. King Saul consulted the prophet Samuel even after Samuel had passed away.[43] "It shows that the people at the time of the prophets believed in the immortality of the soul after the decay of the body," Halevi writes. "For this reason they consulted the dead."[44]

In the Bible, then, the soul lived on but essentially slept eternally. By Second Temple times, death was spoken of as a transition from this life into an everlasting life with God. The soul would now spend eternity conscious, wide awake; and, depending on how honestly and decently the person had lived on earth, the soul would live forever in the presence of its divine maker.

In other words, Judaism embraced from the very begining the concept of *personal judgment*, the idea that individuals are responsible for their own behavior and one day will have to answer for themselves.

But what form would the final judgment take? The Talmud, composed in the centuries after the end of the Second Commonwealth, offered many opinions but settled on none. The rabbis asked the right questions but reached no conclusions; short of a divine voice from heaven, how could they?

What would the afterlife, which Jews called the world-to-come, look like?

The rabbis wanted to know whether one regained one's physical body in the world-to-come. They wondered how physical injuries would be handled; whether people who suffered injuries before death would have their physical wholeness restored. They were curious about clothing and eating in the world-to-come. They also could not determine whether everyone would enjoy the next world, or just Jews, or just righteous Jews, or just learned Jews, or even minimally observant Jews.

And what would people do all day in the world-to-come? Jews steeped in poverty viewed it as a wonderful banquet, where Leviathan—the fabled beast God brought into being during the six days of creation—would be served to them on steaming platters. The ancient rabbis pictured the next world as a vast talmudical academy where God or the prophet Elijah would finally provide answers to all the unanswerable halakhic questions the sages over the centuries had posed. (The one concept of afterlife that never entered Judaism, much to its credit, was a place where you could get endless sexual pleasure if you just killed some enemies of the faith.)

The Talmud, in tractate Sanhedrin, offers some enticing glimpses of the next world. All Israel will have a portion in it, the rabbis promised.[45] They tell us more in Pirke Avot—the tractate known as Ethics of the Fathers: Those who acquire words of Torah obtain life in the world-to-come.[46] The grant of reward to the righteous will come in the next world.[47] The very act of reflecting on the afterlife protects us from coming into the power of sin.[48] This world is like a foyer or lobby in which we prepare ourselves to enter the next world—the main room, as it were.[49] And a fascinating paradox: "More beautiful is one hour of repentance and good deeds in this world than is all of the world-to-come, yet one hour of the blissfulness of spirit in the afterlife is more beautiful than one's entire life in this world."[50]

By the time of the Talmud, therefore, Judaism was convinced that a better world than this one existed, and that Jews could reach it via two different routes. One was to live a good life and gain the world-to-come after one's death; the other was to have the good fortune to be alive when the Messiah comes or to participate in the resurrection of the dead that the Messiah would cause.

But in the latter case, logistical problems arose. How would the dead get to the land of Israel, the presumed location for resurrection? Would their souls travel through the air, or would their bodies make their way to Israel via underground passages? And what would people do in the resurrected state? Would they have to work? Would they run the risk of dying a second time? Was there the possibility of sin in the world after this one?

Even though these questions had no answers, resurrection, judgment, and afterlife gained wide currency among Jews. In fact, resurrection, like mysticism, was an idea that looked better and better as the condition of the Jewish people grew worse and worse. After the close of the Talmud, as Jews dispersed to lands throughout the known world, they often found themselves in desperate political situations with no apparent solution. In those times, the twin concepts of messianic redemption and resurrection of the dead became extremely appealing.

Saadia Gaon, a tenth-century philosopher and rabbinic leader, offered a compelling vision of what life on earth would be like once the Messiah arrived.

Faith in God would be universal, Saadia said; the crippled would be healed; people would live for a long time but not forever; people would desire to do good; and, of pressing concern to Jews crammed into tiny ghettos, everyone would have enough living space, calculated by Saadia to be nearly 288 cubits of ground per person. Saadia even went so far as to predict the arrival of the Messiah in the year 964.[51]

The Messiah, of course, did not arrive in 964. Many rabbis predicted dates for the Messiah's arrival based on mystical calculations. When the Messiah missed each of these appointments, the rabbis generally explained that the arrival of the Messiah was dependent on the good deeds of the people. The Jewish people, their hopes deflated, struggled on.[52]

Two centuries later, Maimonides, the great philosopher, spiritual and political leader, offered his own view of the redeemer.

The Messiah, in Maimonides' mind's eye, would restore Israel's political sovereignty. He would lead the Jews back to Palestine. He would be a great king, more famous even than King Solomon. Jews wait for a Messiah, wrote Maimonides, not because they want prosperity or to ride on horseback[53] or to drink wine. They want God to anoint a new leader for them because with a righteous king, they can concentrate on spirituality.

The ideas of afterlife, messianic redemption, kabbalistic mysticism, and resurrection of the dead, in whatever form that most appealed to the individual Jew, offered hope and solace through bleak and dangerous centuries of Jewish survival. They became vital parts of Jewish belief and, for twenty centuries, provided approaches to a personal relationship with the One God.

These beliefs made it possible to ride out the storms of expulsions, murders, and shattered communities.

*

Orthodox Jews still accept the ideas of judgment, afterlife, resurrection, and the coming of the Messiah. Since the early nineteenth century, though, the newer forms of Judaism—Reform and Conservative Judaism, and more recently Reconstructionist and Humanistic Judaism—do not include some or even all of these beliefs. How well does Judaism survive without these tenets, all of which spring from belief in the continuing existence and care of a loving (and demanding) God?

In some ways, Judaism is doing quite nicely. Jews today prosper and play important roles in business, education, politics and the arts throughout the world. On the other hand, if we look at the question of Jewish *continuity*, we have to ask ourselves how well we're really doing. Obviously the best way to guarantee that one's children will be Jewish is to marry another Jew. But most Jews today do not find compelling arguments for marrying within the faith. Why is that? Why has it become less and less important to maintain one's Jewish identity and to pass it on?

I think it's because so many Jews today don't get good Jewish educations and don't know what Judaism contains. Even those of us who went to Sunday School and Hebrew School weren't taught much about the traditional Jewish concepts and beliefs we've discussed in the last few chapters. We're taught much more about the two hundred year old tradition of *doubt* and very little about the four thousand year old tradition of *faith*.

It makes sense. Contemporary Jewish education reflects the concept of assimilation—the sense that we're better off if we blend in. Of course, even modern Judaism isn't ready to blend in all the way and give up all vestiges of our Jewish nature. We might have a Christmas tree, but we still have that menorah. Nevertheless, today's Judaism doesn't touch too often on the things that made Jews Jews. And the modern concept of Judaism just isn't appealing enough to most Jews today as a set of organizing principles around which to base one's whole life.

If the traditional approach included concepts of a close connection to God, afterlife, resurrection, and a Messiah, and managed to keep Judaism thriving for thousands of years, then what's the nature of current day Judaism, and why can it barely hold our attention?

Would you be surprised if those questions were at the heart of our next chapter?

8

A Fine Mess

Judaism today, outside Orthodoxy, rests on three pillars: affection for the State of Israel, philanthropy, and Holocaust remembrance.

In 1967, when Israel won the Six-Day War, I was nine years old. Even we children grasped that this victory was a miracle approaching biblical proportions. Many Jews literally danced in the streets. One tiny country had defeated six Goliath-sized nations. God had spoken, we thought. Moshe Dayan, a general who shared the name of the leader who had brought the Israelites out of Egypt, led his troops to the Western Wall. Israel could do no wrong. Those who recall the 1967 war remember the sense of excitement and joy that even the mention of the name of the State of Israel evoked.

Times changed. The State of Israel developed a swelled head. Caught by surprise in the Yom Kippur

War of 1973, Israel might have been defeated by the Egyptian army, were it not for American intervention. A sense of malaise descended upon Israel; in its sullen defensiveness, suddenly the state could do nothing right.

Events like the lightning raid on Entebbe, Uganda, on July 4, 1976, to rescue the victims of a jet hijacking, were overshadowed by a long series of public relations gaffes. Israeli military advisors turned up on the evening news, teaching despots all over the world how to fight guerilla wars or maintain political power. The 1982 Lebanon war enmeshed Israel in a Vietnam-like morass. That fall, Israeli soldiers in essence permitted the massacres at Sabra and Shatilla in Lebanon. Lebanese Christian Phalangists killed four hundred sixty Palestinians in refugee relocation camps that should have been protected by Israeli troops. Israel's reputation for morality was heavily tarnished.

The Jewish state's reputation for living by a higher ethical standard took a beating twice more in the 1980s. First, many Americans, both Jews and Gentiles, were offended by Israel's complicity in the Oliver North arms-for-hostages deal, but the political and legal issues raised by Iran-Contra were fundamentally of concern only to Americans. Israel's involvement was quite secondary and was intended, at least in part, as a quid pro quo for the well-being of Iran's remaining Jewish community, but few people remember that aspect of the situation.

Second was the intifada, the Palestinian uprising in the occupied Gaza and West Bank regions. Night after night, evening news audiences witnessed Israeli soldiers using force against civilian demonstrators, many of whom were teenagers or even children.

Israel responded that the leaders of the intifada were callously and purposely using youngsters as front-line fighters to put Israel in a bad light; that the Palestinian provocations, as a serious threat to public safety and order, required a military response; and that Israel was the only democracy in the Middle East and certainly the only nation there that would permit television cameras to witness civil strife. Unfortunately, arguments of this complexity did not lend themselves to TV sound-bites.

Israel had always been David to the Arab Goliath; now, in the popular mind, the roles had been reversed. Much of the news coverage was slanted against Israel and horribly one-sided. But the net effect was to deprive Israel of much of the respect, and good will it had commanded around the world only a generation before.

If anything, the peace process of the 1990s has reduced even further the importance of the State of Israel in the minds of young Jews. Without a sense of crisis to focus attention, many young Jews feel that the situation is under control and that the Israel will get by without their attention or involvement.

Zionism no longer excites Jewish passions the way it once did. As part of the "trinity" of modern Jewish awareness, along with the Holocaust and philanthropy, Zionism no longer casts the same magic spell. In short, while the State of Israel remains dear to Jews everywhere, enthusiasm about it no longer offers young people a vital reason to identify spiritually as Jews.

Philanthropy, the second tenet of modern Judaism, has, of course, a long history in the Jewish faith; the whole notion of tithing, of giving a percentage of one's income to charity, dates back to Sinai. But philanthropy requires a sense that one charity is more deserving than another. Fundraisers for Jewish organizations must compete against alumni campaigns, legal defense funds, medical research, disaster relief, arts groups, public radio and television, political campaigns, and a host of other good causes.

Throughout our history, Jews always cemented their Jewishness with philanthropy; even the poorest of the poor traditionally gave each other what little they could spare. Jewish groups could always count on Jews for support. Today, as the sense of Jewish identity grows more and more tenuous, Jewish organizations of every kind are hurting. Philanthropy in support of Jewish causes is no longer, in and of itself, a meaningful link to Judaism for young Jews.

The third aspect of modern Judaism is Holocaust remembrance. A shared sense of horror and loss linked all Jews for the first half-century after the end of World War II. Today, though, as the Holocaust recedes in popular memory, as denial that the Holocaust took place gains believers even on mainstream university campuses, and as the last generation of survivors pass, the Holocaust has begun to lose the urgent sense of relevance it once possessed. It's very hard, in any case, to ask young people to dedicate their lives to the following proposition: "Fifty years ago, Jews were killed because they were Jewish. I am Jewish, so to honor their memory I should become more Jewishly involved. I should only date or marry other Jews."

That's simply too great a leap of logic to ask young people to make. And yet, modern Judaism casts itself in terms of a connection to a morally average State of Israel, the writing of checks to Jewish organizations that are hard-pressed to demonstrate that they are more relevant to the lives of young Jews than, say, National Public Radio, and loyalty to the remembrance of an event that shocks the conscience but—whether Jewish leaders care to admit it—loses its historical relevance in the minds of young Jews with each passing year.

These three ideas—Zionism, philanthropy, and Holocaust remembrance—the "trinity" of modern secular Judaism, are simply inadequate to address the spiritual needs of Jews. It's no wonder, therefore, that Jews either go through life talking to God three times a year or look elsewhere to get their spiritual needs fulfilled.

(Ironically, as those who work with religious Christians can attest, Gentiles admire Jews who stand up for the precepts of their own faith. Let me offer a wonderful illustration of this fact. One time, when I worked for a law firm run by a devout Catholic, the head of the firm and an attorney met with a client who demanded a lengthy series of documents for a transaction set to close the day after Rosh Hashanah, the Jewish New Year.

The head of the firm, whom I will call Mr. Collins, noticed that the lawyer in charge of producing those documents, an Orthodox Jew whom I will call Mr. Josephson, had begun to squirm. Mr. Collins knew that the Jewish calendar dictated the presence of Mr. Josephson in synagogue for the next two days and not behind his desk.

Mr. Collins turned to the client, who, as it happened, also was Jewish, and said: "Mr. Josephson is an Orthodox Jew and he does not work over the Jewish New Year. So you'll have those documents not on Monday but by the middle of next week. By the way, you're Jewish, aren't you? How come you're planning to work on the Jewish New Year?"

Mr. Collins became a hero to those of us who knew this story. The point of recounting it is simply to indicate that many Gentiles respect Jews who observe the precepts of Judaism. Christians do not expect Jews to be Christians; they expect them to be Jews.[54])

Even some modern Reform Jewish leaders recognize that something important was lost when so many of the ancient tenets of Judaism were lost. "I do not love Reform services," writes William Blank in an essay entitled "Why a Reform Rabbi Davens [Prays] in a Conservative Shul [Temple]." "They move me only a little. I do not love responsive readings in English, organs, creative services . . . unison . . . where you can't get up and walk around in the middle. . . . I prefer traditional davening [prayer]."[55]

At services utilizing the Reform *Union Prayer Book*, relates author Mark Lee Raphael, "worshippers were usually prayed for, preached to, and sung at."[56] Adds Elliot Strom, another Reform thinker: "We have lost the sense of majesty and splendor that earlier typified our classical Reform worship, and this is tragic."[57]

The problem is much broader than the way in which modern Reform services are conducted, however. Judaism, which lost its spiritual moorings a hundred and fifty years ago, faces some serious problems, and no one really wants to talk about them.

The first problem is that *nobody cares*. By the mid-1980s, as many as thirty-five percent of American Jews surveyed agreed with the statement that "religion is not very important" in their lives—in contrast to only 14 per cent of the general population.[58] That figure jibes with the eight percent regular synagogue attendance I mentioned earlier on.

Intermarriage, a traditional barometer of affiliation in Judaism, has skyrocketed in the twentieth century. From 1900 until 1920, only two percent of Jews married out. From 1940 to 1960, six percent did so. From 1960 to 1965, seventeen percent of Jews married Gentiles. By the 1980s, the figure had reached thirty-two percent.[59] Writes sociologist Neil Sandberg: "As Jews leave their families, friends, and neighborhoods to pursue careers in the modern world, the cohesiveness of the Jewish community is weakened. . . . There are social and psychological costs associated with mobility."[60]

Marrying another Jew does not guarantee that one's children will care about their Jewishness, but two Jews marrying certainly offers the greatest likelihood of such an outcome. Intermarriage in the United States has now passed the fifty percent mark; in the Los Angeles area more than seventy percent of Jews marry non-Jews. According to a 1990 study, "[F]or every new couple consisting of two Jewish partners, there were approximately two new couples in which only one of the partners was Jewish."[61] Once, Jews married out for social or business opportunities; today, they do so because they were never given a sense that there was anything important about being Jewish.

The second problem is that the only people who know or care about the beliefs and philosophies of Reform and Conservative Judaism are either Reform or Conservative rabbis or currently in rabbinical school.

Most rank-and-file Reform or Conservative Jews today belong because their parents belonged. Their parents often joined because they were looking for a "halfway-house" kind of Judaism—halfway between Orthodoxy and no affiliation at all. Belonging to a Reform or Conservative temple can be a means of maintaining a sense of Jewish identity without really having to do much.

The two largest branches of Judaism may well be afraid of their congregants and big donors. Marshall Sklare, author of the definitive book on Conservative Judaism, quotes a disgruntled Conservative rabbi who points out that the movement has not sanctioned deviations from traditional Jewish practice, yet "in the eyes of the layman, [it] stands for the rights to be *mchallel Shabbat* [one who does not observe the Sabbath] and to eat *treyfot* [nonkosher food].[62] If Conservative and Reform Judaism ever tried to enforce religious expectations on donors and congregants, the results would likely not be favorable.

Some of our largest congregations have turned into vast Bar and Bat Mitzvah mills where, as author Helen Jeiven suggests, the "bar" may be bigger than the "mitzvah."[63] An expert on planning Bar Mitzvahs, Jeiven decries the inanities that some parents insist upon: chimpanzees that can skate, *a cappella* singers who stroll among the tables and take requests.[64]

Children cannot be fooled; they sense intuitively what's going on when the quality of the teaching drops off precipitously on Sunday mornings compared to their weekday classes in public school. Children know that some sort of fraud is happening when they are taught to parrot Hebrew words that neither they, their friends, nor their parents understand or even care about. They are taught a religion of "not" (with examples all couched in the past tense): Jews kept the Sabbath, but not us; Jews kept kosher, but not us; Jews put on tefillin or kept Jewish holidays, but not us.

Jewish children attending the typical Jewish Sunday school in America are often taught to be schizophrenic about Judaism. They are placed, against their will, in a powerful and terrible double bind: they are told, "This is what Jews have always done. Even though you're a Jew, don't do it. Just be sure you marry another Jew."

If the parents are bored, shnorred, and ignored, the children feel used, confused, and unamused. Used because they are placed at the center of a religious observance without a real explanation of what the whole thing is about. Confused because children instinctively prefer honesty to hypocrisy; the "Jews do this but we don't" routine is distasteful to Jews of any age. And unamused. Adult Jews who are lighthearted and fun-loving invariably grow solemn when they explain to you why, as a Jewish friend of mine in his early thirties put it, "my spirituality has nothing to do with my religion."

Jews who intermarry are not running away from God or even Judaism. They are escaping the confusing Alice in Wonderland religion they were taught; and I don't blame them.

The third problem is that the leaders and leading authors of the various groups were for many decades too busy taking potshots at one another to stop and acknowledge the terrible divisions that the Jewish people now face. The border between tragedy and farce is always thin. The criticisms the various branches of Judaism launch at each other would be laughable if they did not symbolize the bitterness among the groups.

Some examples: The Reform say of the Orthodox:

"Orthodoxy, which has failed to win the allegiance of most of [Israel's] own citizenry, will not exert any real influence upon the spiritual life of Jews elsewhere."[65] The Orthodox fire back: the reformers are "traitors to their people, their land, and their God,"[66] and their Judaism is an expression of "deviance."[67] Conservative institutions in Israel, Sklare writes, are "barely tolerated" by the Orthodox.[68] And on and on, while another non-Orthodox writer predicts Orthodoxy's "demise."[69]

And the pews in synagogues and temples continue to empty out, and the intermarriage rate keeps rising, and the leaders fiddle while Rome burns.

Where have the Orthodox been while all this has been going on? Merely defying all predictions of their imminent demise. Orthodox Judaism is one of the great religious success stories of the century. Everyone expected that traditional Judaism would die out in the years following World War II. It did not happen that way. Orthodoxy is in the midst of a massive resurgence. Its members have a strong commitment to practicing Judaism on a day-to-day basis. They still believe in the religious concepts that Reform removed from its approach to Judaism: daily prayer from the traditional prayer book; lifelong study of Talmud, commentaries, and other traditional literature; ritual observance; Messiah, resurrection, and afterlife; and most important, observance of Jewish law, which provides constant contact with the One God.

They also have large families. Orthodoxy may have far fewer adherents than the non-Orthodox denominations, but they marry early, start families early, and have lots of children. Their educational institutions are thriving. They will never outnumber the non-Orthodox Jews, but from their point of view, they do not need to. To the extent that they think about non-Orthodox Jews, the Orthodox essentially pity them and consider them irrelevant to Judaism's future. In the words of Rabbi Joseph Soloveitchik, one of twentieth-century Orthodoxy's most influential thinkers, "If a man was not privileged to be born into a religious home—or to have developed a religious sensibility through our education—he does not deserve our ire but rather our sympathy and pity."[70]

To the Orthodox, non-Orthodox, nonobservant, and nonaffiliated Jews are barely Jews at all. Orthodoxy sees itself as a modern-day Noah's Ark sailing calmly across a sea of assimilation. Orthodoxy identifies strongly with the saving-remnant theory of Judaism. After every major disaster in Jewish history, from the destruction of the First Temple in 586 B.C.E. to the destruction of the European Jewish community in the Holocaust, a tiny remnant of survivors dusted itself off and recommitted to the One God. The Orthodox, who make up less than two million of the world's thirteen million Jews, see themselves as the only Jews in our time who will survive as Jews. The non-Orthodox, they believe, will intermarry, assimilate, and simply drop off the face of the Jewish map.

The Orthodox define commitment to Judaism in terms of Torah and mitzvot, the Bible and the commandments. If you do not observe Jewish law, they believe, then chances are that your children will marry out and their children will not even be Jewish.

For the most part, the Orthodox are unconcerned about their secular and non-Orthodox brothers and sisters. Their Noah's Ark has already left the pier, and with only a few exceptions, the gangplank is up. A few Orthodox groups have founded schools that introduce young adults to traditional Judaism. If you stand in front of the Western Wall in Jerusalem long enough, you will probably be invited to visit one. It is possible, but not easy, for a Jew from a nonobservant upbringing to enter Orthodoxy and find acceptance there. A small number of Jews make the journey, and, most likely, an equally small number leave Orthodoxy in any given year. By and large, though, we see little movement across the chasm that has begun to separate Orthodoxy from the rest of Judaism.

Yet Orthodoxy itself is hardly the monolith that most non-Orthodox Jews assume it to be. The last twenty years have witnessed a shift in power in the Orthodox world to the hard right. Much of Jewish practice and belief is a matter of interpretation; it is easy to justify any of a variety of approaches to most laws or customs within the complex world of Jewish thought. Lately, a small number of influential Orthodox leaders have staked out increasingly hard-line positions for themselves and their adherents. All of Orthodoxy finds itself pulled to the right or forced to explain the reason why. As Orthodoxy moves rightward, it moves, of course, further and further away from the rest of Judaism.

This turn to the right touches virtually every aspect of traditional Jewish life. Take weddings. At an Orthodox Jewish wedding in the 1950s, there might have been ballroom dancing. Time passed and the genders began to dance separately, in large circles on different parts of the dance floor. Then came separate seating for the men and the women during the wedding service. And then, in right-wing Orthodox circles, came the innovation of a *mechitzah*, a physical barrier, between the men's and women's sections so that no one could even see the opposite sex during the entire event.

Similarly, an Orthodox Jewish male might not have worn his yarmulke to college or to work in the 1950s or 1960s. Today his son will wear his yarmulke anywhere and probably not take a job if he cannot wear it. Orthodox Jews forty years ago might have eaten fish "out"— that is, in nonkosher restaurants; in today's Orthodox world, one finds much less tolerance for actions that violate Jewish law.

Orthodoxy is too caught up in the throes of its own rightward pull to worry about what the non-Orthodox Jewish world is up to. And to assimilated, secular, Humanistic, Reconstructionist, Reform, and Conservative Jews, Orthodoxy is virtually irrelevant.

My greatest fear is that Judaism is on the verge of a schism; a complete and painful splitting in two. Sparks fly every so often when an individual converted to Judaism by a non-Orthodox rabbi seeks to marry or adopt children in Israel.[71] The Orthodox relent only when large donors to Israel in the West tighten the screws and threaten a massive cutoff of financial aid. But these small flare-ups indicative of the gulf between the Orthodox and the non-Orthodox are *trivial,* I fear, compared to what's coming.

I would not be surprised if, in the next twenty years or so, a few Orthodox rabbis actually declare it illegal under Jewish law for an Orthodox Jew to marry a non-Orthodox Jew, with the offspring of such a forbidden union to carry the stigma of *mamzerut* or illegitimacy. The parents of Orthodox Jews who marry outside Orthodoxy will be required to comply with the mourning customs that parents of Jews who marry Gentiles today observe.

This may sound unbelievable, but as the schism between Orthodoxy and non-Orthodoxy widens, it is only a matter of time before one side or the other codifies it and makes it a matter of Jewish law. The two groups already live in two different worlds with only a limited amount of overlap. The Orthodox run their lives by the Jewish calendar, do not work or travel on the Sabbath, eat only kosher food and in kosher restaurants, attend synagogue regularly—in many cases, daily. They educate their children with a priority on Jewish matters. While many modern or centrist Orthodox parents send their children to college, some do not want their children to come in contact with the secular ideas and mores found on university campuses.

Many right-wing Orthodox Jews do not even have televisions in their homes. They look at modern culture with the same combination of shock and disdain that they believe God must have felt on viewing Sodom. Orthodox Jews do not perceive any present-day crisis in Judaism. They believe that there *was* a crisis—the question of whether Orthodoxy was going to survive modern times. This view is exemplified by the following quotation from a recent Orthodox commentary on the Book of Lamentations: "How much of our fall is due to...Jewish intelligentsia and movements that thought the millennium could be found outside of Torah life?"[72]

Everyone assumed that old-fashioned Judaism could never survive in the United States. Everyone was wrong. Orthodoxy is in beautiful shape these days. Its adherents feel triumphant, having proved wrong those who predicted its demise.

It may be only a matter of time, therefore, before some Orthodox authority seeks to solemnize the divorce between the Orthodox and the rest of the world's Jews. This would be one of the greatest tragedies ever to befall the Jewish people. We have enough problems without bringing on our own civil war.

To sum up, there is a monstrously large crisis facing Judaism today. The question is not, will the Jewish people survive? Most likely we will. The question is what form that survival will take. The future of the Orthodox is assured. And there are so many millions of non-Orthodox Jews in the world that simply on a numerical basis, even if sixty percent continued to intermarry, and even if none of the children of those intermarriages identifies as Jewish, there would still be plenty of Jews left.

The question is, how can Jews for whom Orthodoxy is not an option find spiritual sustenance in their own faith, and find a way to pass on to children a sense that one's Jewishness matters?

As long as temples function as Bar and Bat Mitzvah mills, unwilling or unable to tell Jewish young people what Judaism actually stands for, as long as Judaism defines itself as devotion to the State of Israel, philanthropy, and Holocaust remembrance, as long as Jews leave religious services feeling bored, shnorred, and ignored, Judaism will continue to fail Jews.

Why have the Orthodox survived and thrived when other modern forms of Judaism really fail to hold the attention of their members? My answer to this vital question probably won't surprise you. The Orthodox, more than any other form of Judaism today, devote themselves to God. They maintain the beliefs that other kinds of Judaism don't always accept—afterlife, judgment, Messiah, resurrection. They don't necessarily focus all day long on these ideas. But they kept those ideas alive. And those ideas, in turn, keep the Orthodox alive. And they educate their children about the ideas we've been discussing in this book. And their children grow up with a much stronger attachment to Judaism.

Long-term survival of Judaism requires Jews interested enough in their heritage to pass it on to their children. All the statistics regarding non-Orthodox Judaism today—intermarriage, synagogue membership, service attendance, or Jewish education level—point to a hollow shell. No one wants to say that Judaism is failing, but isn't it? We have institutions, organizations, schools...but are they really making the grade? Truthfully? In what ways can we honestly judge today's non-Orthodox Judaism a success?

Orthodoxy simply isn't for everyone. That's indisputable. The question then becomes this: is there any way to strengthen the other forms of Judaism today so that they, and their adherents, have a better chance of succeeding?

We've tried, for the past hundred fifty years, to create successful forms of Judaism that don't rely on God. To go back to the point we discussed in the beginning, if a religious system *doesn't* start with a notion of God, how can it possibly satisfy? How can you get the answers to ultimate issues without some form of ultimate authority? And if we *are* Jewish, why do we limit ourselves only to the approach of the last few generations, for whom rationalism and assimilationism were the test? Why can't we really know, teach, explore, and live by, the ideas that held Judiasm together for millenia?

Is there a solution? Of course. Besiege your rabbi or community leader. Show him or her this book and demand to know more about the Jewish view of God. Explain that you are completely dissatisfied with deadening services. Withhold your contributions—and your children—until they get the message. What do the rabbis and leaders have to lose? The eight percent of Jews who still attend. And don't you think that the eight percent would be even happier with Judaism if it were God-based and not based primarily on Zionism, check-writing, and Holocaust remembrance (as important as each of these three concepts is)?

And you can do one more thing right now to develop your own sense of authentic Jewish spirituality. You can take your feelings and your questions and your desires for a sense of spiritual connectedness right to the top. You yourself can have a relationship with the One God, with the Jewish God, with the God of your ancestors.

And you can begin to build that relationship . . . right now.

How to go about doing it—how to be Jewish despite the way Judaism is currently established—is at the heart of the next chapter.

9

You and God

Abraham Joshua Heschel writes that there are three ways to know God, three "trails," as he puts it: worship, learning, and action.[73] Perhaps one or more of these trails might be useful for you.

The first trail, worship involves prayer and meditation. Prayer is where you talk to God; meditation is where you listen for an answer. We will discuss each of these concepts in a moment. First, though, let's take a brief look at the ideas of learning and action.

The second trail, learning, can mean reading more books, listening to tapes, attending classes, or forming discussion groups. Many people today join book clubs to talk about current novels. But how much more would you benefit if you set aside even one evening a month to meditate or talk with your friends about spiritual matters.

You might even consider reading the Bible all the way through, a few pages every morning or every evening. If you have not looked into the Bible since your religious school days, you might find that the events and personalities described therein mean much more now that you are encountering them as an adult. If you know it only from secular college study, you may find that reading it from a spiritual perspective makes a world of difference. Although Mark Twain defined a classic as a book which people praise and don't read, there must be something to the Bible that accounts for the longevity of its popularity not just among Jews but for everyone.

Heschel's third trail to God, action, takes on a variety of forms in Judaism. Action can refer to the fulfillment of rituals, the observance of the Sabbath and holidays, and obedience to the commandments set forth in the Bible. It can also refer to the other ways Jews have traditionally found God: through service, and through decency of character.

People often ask, "But if I'm an ethical person, isn't that enough?" The answer in traditional Judaism is that having a good character is necessary but not sufficient to be a complete Jew. In order to transmit decency to our children, we have to be decent ourselves. And to transmit Judaism to our children, we have to know *Judaism* ourselves. Hence this paragraph from the Talmud which for two thousand years Jews have repeated as part of their morning prayers:

> "The following are things of which you enjoy the interest in this world while the principal is held for your benefit in the world-to-come: honoring father and mother; performing acts of kindness; arriving early at the house of study morning and evening; offering guests hospitality; visiting the sick; providing dowries for brides; attending funerals; mindfulness in prayer; and making peace between individuals; but the study of Torah is equivalent to all of these things."[74]

Goodness, the Talmud tells us, is sufficient to transmit goodness, but without knowledge of Judaism, we cannot transmit Judaism. We cannot give away what we don't have. And in an era when organized Judaism does not take seriously its responsibility to teach Judaism to Jews, that responsibility falls upon Jews as individuals.

What Jewish laws to observe and how to observe them are questions to which dozens of excellent books address themselves. Our time together focuses more on the question of why we observe; of what it means to be an heir to the magnificent Jewish spiritual tradition. You get to choose your own path or paths to God.

Let's talk about prayer.

I'm going to ask you to take three steps with me down a trail that leads to God. My job is simply to guide you onto the trail, and then you can follow it for as long as you like. But we'll take these first three steps together. I want to help you reconsider your ideas about God. The first step is to move from the idea of God as a "taker" to God as a "giver."

The second step is to move from doubt to faith.

The third step is to move from the idea of God as distant to the idea of God as present.

Let's begin.

Is God a giver or a taker? In our secular world, we most keenly sense the presence of God at funerals. We lose someone we love; we watch them lowered into the ground, covered up, never to return to us. At such moments we think of God as a taker.

But we never focus on the idea that if God has taken that person from us, then perhaps God gave us that person in the first place. We never think that the gifts we enjoy actually have a source. As a child, you were probably trained to thank people for things they gave you—birthday presents, compliments, Bar or Bat Mitzvah checks. I once dropped in at the house of some close friends. Their son, then four years old, was sitting in the foyer.

"Hey, whaddya say?" I said to my little friend.

He pondered the question for a moment, and asked, in reply, "Thank you?"

We are socialized even, perhaps, from the age of four to express gratitude for the gifts in our lives. I suggest that you begin to think about God—the One God, the God of Abraham, the same God who created the universe, the stars, and the planets; I respectfully suggest that you begin to consider the idea, if you haven't already, that God is the Being who not only causes lives to end but gave you your life, your very existence on earth, as an act of love.

Sometimes people think of spirituality as a state of heightened awareness. In this state you might ask yourself whether you are fully aware of the stunning miracle that your life represents. Consider it now: There are forty trillion cells in your body, all of which are filled with intelligence, all of which communicate with one another in a vast, stunning, silent harmony. You have the gifts of respiration, mobility, the senses, the ability to experience pleasure, whether emotional, physical, sexual. You have the ability to think, read, write, communicate, make connections among ideas, understand concepts.

Simple fairness suggests that if we blame God for taking the lives of people we love, we ought to thank God for giving us our own lives and the lives of those around us.

Death itself makes sense if we think of it as the tax we pay for loving someone. Our modern culture has a particular horror of death for at least three reasons.

First, we live in a youth culture. Why? Because advertisers know that younger people are more likely to adopt or switch brands of apparel, personal care products, tires, or food more than older people, so they emphasize the young in their ads. Second, we have so little faith in the idea of a hereafter, in which Jews have believed since the beginning of our faith.

And third, because the American way of death—hospitalization, tubes, oxygen tanks, and antiseptic, unfamiliar surroundings—is such a horrible way to end our time on earth.

Other cultures and societies accept death as a part of the natural cycle; Jews in the past always did, as one discovers when reading the Bible and Talmud. But if we begin to see our entire lives as gifts from God, if we see God in every fiber of our being and in our awareness of the magnificent beauty of our planet, in our capacities to love and be loved, to help others and to accept help—if we see God in our lives, we stop seeing God as an enemy when a loved one dies.

Yes, God takes. Over the course of a lifetime, all of us will lose people and things we love, and there will be no apparent meaning or explanation for those losses.

But God gives. God gives all the time. Why do we see God's presence only in disaster and crisis, so-called acts of God? Is a sunset or a chrysanthemum any less an act of God than an earthquake or a flood?

Isn't it interesting, by the way, how we blame God for the destruction that earthquakes and floods cause us, although we become their victims only because we ourselves have chosen to live in areas that we know to be earthquake- or flood-prone? We spend so much time blaming God for the results of the choices we make, and so little time expressing gratitude for the gifts we enjoy every day of our lives.

What we give our attention to, grows. We can cultivate an attitude of gratitude the same way gardeners cultivate roses—with passionate attention. Go out today and buy a spiral notebook and start a "gratitude list." Begin by writing down ten things for which you are grateful. Every night, before you go to bed, add three more items to your list. The items can be things like "My marriage" or "My kids" or "My English professor" or "My dog" or a good movie you saw or a good book you read or a happy or joyful experience you had with someone else. Write down more than three things if you like. This simple act of daily acknowledgement of gratitude for the gifts you enjoy, combined with an acknowledgement of the true source of those gifts, can turn around your entire attitude toward life.

Of course God takes. It's all God's to begin with. But God gives. Your happiness will be in direct proportion to your ability to recognize the true source of the wonderful gifts in your life.

Thinking of God as a giver and not just a taker asks us to revise many of the attitudes about God that seep into our lives from a variety of sources. Accepting the notion of God as a loving, giving friend requires us to dismiss from our minds the way others, from televangelists to terrorists, abuse the idea of God. Despite the impression they convey, God is not a prop to wave around in order to solicit donations or sympathy for ungodly causes.

Of course they are free to do whatever they like with their concept of God; like us, they have free will. But we don't have to let the ways some people use God for fundraising or political purposes stand in the way of our new, deepening relationship with the One God.

I was once at a political rally in California during a presidential campaign. The president and vice-president of the United States were sitting on the dais while a world-famous televangelist gave the invocation. He began with a joke: "This is the kind of party God would throw—if He had the money!"

Everyone laughed, and I have to admit that it was a pretty good one-liner. But if we make God the butt of our jokes, can we really turn around a moment later and address God as—well, as God?

During the invocation itself, the televangelist asked God for the election of several candidates running for local office in Orange County, just south of Los Angeles. Is that really what God wants? For us to pray for the election of specific city managers or district attorneys? "There is an idolatry, it seems to me, in being so sure that we know God's political will," writes rabbi and commentator Arthur Hertzberg.[75] We do not have to let the ways other people "use" God affect the way we understand God.

We live in a Christian society, and certain aspects of Christian belief naturally filter through the environment. There is nothing in the Bible, for example, suggesting that angels have wings, halos, or harps, but if I asked you to describe an angel, you would include some or all of those features. Angels exist in the Bible; they serve as messengers and as protectors.

They do have wings—at least so say Isaiah and Ezekiel.[76] But they don't have harps. And they certainly don't have halos.

Similarly, if you ask Jewish children whose grandparents have died where their grandparents now live, the typical response would be, of course, "heaven." Well, as we have seen, Judaism has always accepted the idea of an afterlife, but never thought of it as heaven. We call it the world-to-come, and sometimes *Gan Eden*, Hebrew for "Garden of Eden."

Yet many Jews have unconsciously embraced the idea that when you die, you go to heaven, even though Judaism has never located its afterlife there. How many times have you heard one Jew tell another a story involving St. Peter and the pearly gates? We don't have a St. Peter, and we don't have pearly gates.

These are comparatively minor matters. Some more important ideas that we have unwittingly adopted from certain of our Gentile neighbors are the beliefs that human beings are inherently sinful, that pleasure is wrong, and that happiness cannot and should not be pursued in this life. Judaism is all about the recognition of the potential for joyfulness and happiness in everything that we do. The same Hebrew expression that means "fear of God," *yirat shamayim*, also means awe.

The Jew stands with a sense of wonder, joy, and excitement about life and the possibility of a close relationship with God. A sage in the Jerusalem Talmud suggests that when our lives come to a close, we will be asked to explain why we didn't try to find more joy and delight in life.[77] For a people so downtrodden in history, we are astonishingly committed to the pursuit of real happiness.

Again, Heschel: "Nowhere in the Bible is found any indication of the idea that the soul is imprisoned in a corrupt body, that to seek satisfaction in this world means to lose one's soul or to forfeit the covenant with God, that the allegiance to God demands renunciation of worldly goods."[78]

We are not "fallen" creatures. The idea that the human race is tainted with original sin is not now and never has been a Jewish idea. We do not look on sex as a bad thing; indeed, the Talmud is quite specific about the duty to give one's partner adequate sexual pleasure.[79] The priests who served in the First and Second Temples were permitted to marry; according to Jewish law, the high priest had to be married.[80] The more you learn about Judaism, the more you see that it is a way to enjoy life and find satisfaction. It's not a hair shirt. Nor is it a penance.

It's easier, then, to think of God as a giver if we make a conscious effort to dismiss from our minds the political, religious, and, frankly, unfair uses to which other people sometimes put the idea of God.

And as you begin to give your attention to the idea of the One God, the God of Israel, as giver, you will find it easier—and actually desirable—to have an awareness of God as a regular part of your life. The next step down the trail is the move from doubt to faith. I admit it; this can be a pretty big step.

Or maybe not. It just depends, once again, on where you wish to place your emphasis and your attention.

As a Jew in the modern world, you are heir to two different Jewish traditions, one less than two hundred years old, and one that stretches back more than three thousand years.

The modern tradition starts with the idea of doubt. Freud and Marx doubted the existence of God. Your parents may have doubted it also. Even your rabbi may have doubted or even denied that there ever was a God.[81] And every time we pick up a newspaper or watch the news on television, and look at all the murder and war and cruelty, we too may wonder whether those who deny the existence of God may not be right.

And then we have to remember that we are not being fair if we blame God for the choices people make, for the bad things people do. The world's conception of God—not just Judaism's—is that God gave us free will because without the capacity to do the wrong thing, we could never choose to do the right thing. As I said in an earlier chapter, God may owe us an explanation for why the world was created this way, but it is not likely to arrive in this lifetime.

So we have a legacy of doubt, which began two centuries ago and seems to be the dominant idea among secular Jews today.

But alongside the legacy of doubt is another approach to thinking about the world. For thousands of years, from Abraham until the Enlightenment, Jews believed there was a God. They may not have understood what God was doing, or may not always have liked the results, but they believed. Dissenting movements often arose in Judaism. The Essenes were a fringe sect who lived in the desert at Qumran, near Jericho and the Dead Sea. The Sadducees adhered only to the written text of the Bible and disputed the claim that God had also conveyed an "oral law" to Moses during his forty days atop Mount Sinai.

The dissenting voices in Judaism's long history did not doubt the existence of God; they simply understood God in a different way.

So as a Jew you are heir to two legacies. For the past hundred and fifty years, outside the Orthodox world, many Jews have doubted the existence of God. For the past four thousand years, most Jews accepted that the world has a creator just the same way that a sculpture has a sculptor.

You are not bound by the last hundred and fifty years of Jewish intellectual history. You are free to explore the question of whether God exists, and you are not bound to accept the conclusions of any previous generation.

As I mentioned earlier, if you are looking for proof that God exists, the Bible will probably not help you. It does not contain any proofs of God's existence. "There are no proofs for the existence of the God of Abraham," writes Heschel. "There are only witnesses." Two million witnesses—the two million witnesses who were physically present at Mount Sinai. Two million witnesses to the presence and speaking voice of God. Two million witnesses, and, as I said earlier, no minority report.

Just because a lot of time has passed does not mean that an event did not happen as the contemporaneous witnesses described it. One of the saddest developments in modern Jewish life is that those who claim the Holocaust never happened are gaining credibility, even among intelligent people In the years immediately after the Holocaust, even Jews could not believe that such a thing had taken place. Eyewitness testimony from credible witnesses—survivors, soldiers, even General Dwight Eisenhower, who visited one of the camps soon after it was liberated—made the Holocaust real in the minds of Jew and non-Jew alike.

How ironic: a people so fearful that a thoroughly witnessed event may be wiped from history by a handful of individuals who claim that it never took place are willing to perform the same sort of historical revisionism in regard to what happened at Mount Sinai. The revelation at Sinai was not a religious event, it was a historical event. Even if it did not happen exactly as written in the Book of Exodus, it's clear, nonetheless, that something enormously powerful took place before the entire community of the children of Israel, something so powerful that the Jewish people continues to exist thousands of years after every other nation in existence at the time disappeared and was lost to history.

The Passover Haggadah suggests that we must each regard ourselves as though we, too, were present at Mount Sinai. But what does that mean?

It means that if we want to take Judaism seriously, we can give our attention to the older of our two legacies, our legacy of faith. We may consider the possibility that the Bible, that stodgy old book that nobody reads, might be a book of history and not simply an outdated collection of myths. Granted, we are technologically more advanced than they were. But maybe they knew a few things that we have forgotten.

The easiest way to move from doubt to faith is to try talking to God as if you really believe that God exists and will pay attention to your prayer. Does God "need" your prayer or my prayer? Hardly. Prayer does not remind God that there is a God. Prayer reminds us that there is a God.

We need constant reminding of this fact, because in our hectic, abrasive, violent world it is so easy to lose sight of anything beyond the next piece of work we have to do, the next telephone message we have to return, the next errand we have to run. Taking time out to pray reminds us that the world is bigger than us and our problems, that we are more than workers or bill payers or runners of errands.

The act of prayer affirms that life has a meaning greater than anything we can understand, and that the more attention we give to the spiritual, the more our life will mean to us.

If you are not accustomed to talking to God, what do you say to start the conversation?

One good way to begin is with the words, "If you're up there."

Start with "If you're up there . . ." and then say all the things you would say to God if you were absolutely certain that God exists. "If you're up there, I'd like you to know . . ." and tell God everything. If you have been angry at God for a long time, you can tell that. If your God cannot handle your anger, you need a bigger God.

Try this even for three minutes a day for the next two weeks. Judaism traditionally has placed a stronger emphasis on action and behavior than on thought. This is why most books about Judaism, even including the Talmud, seem to be more interested in telling you what to do rather than why you should do it. Judaism recognizes a central aspect of human nature: the actions we take, strongly influence the way we think. Judaism is a religion of action. Taking time to pray attaches us to God. Prayer changes us. It changes the way we look at our world and our place in it.

If you want to move from doubt to faith, you have to take at least the smallest action. It's hard to think oneself into faith, because thinking has to do with our capacity to reason, and faith means accepting ideas that are beyond reason. Even for three minutes a day every day for two weeks, talk to God as you would to a loving parent or a loving friend. Express your emotions. God can handle them. Express your gratitude and see how doing so affects you. Make faith your starting point, not your finish line.

Writes Heschel: "There is no word in Biblical Hebrew for doubt; there are many expressions of wonder. Just as . . . our starting point is doubt, wonder is the Biblical starting point in facing reality. . . . Doubt is an act in which the mind inspects its own ideas; wonder is an act in which the mind confronts the universe."[83]

But is it all right for Jews to just talk to God? Don't we have to "go through channels"—don't we have to pray in Hebrew in a synagogue or temple?

Aryeh Kaplan explains:

"It seems that, in general, Jews pray spontaneously less than non-Jews, at least nowadays. There seems to be a feeling that Jewish prayer must be in Hebrew, in a prescribed manner, with a predetermined wording. Many Jews are surprised to learn that there is an unbroken tradition of spontaneous prayer in the Jewish religion. If we look at the spectrum of Jewish literature, we find numerous references to spontaneous personal prayer. Many great Jewish leaders considered their own prayers to be very important to their spiritual development. And in Europe, it was the most natural thing in the world for Jews to cry out to God in their native Yiddish."[84]

Perhaps you might like to take some quiet time every morning, as Jews have done for thousands of years, and focus on your Jewishness, on the miracle of your own existence, on the beauty and wonder that life contains, if we would only take notice. Use prayer—talking to God—as a means of attaching yourself to God and attaching God to you. But start right now. As the old joke goes, God loves to hear from strangers.

The last step we will take together on our trail is the step from God as a distant figure to God as a presence. We begin with Heschel's words:

"The pious man is possessed by his awareness of the presence and the nearness of God. Everywhere and at all times he lives as in His sight, whether he remains always heedful of His proximity or not. He feels embraced by God's mercy as by a vast encircling space. Awareness of God is as close to him as the throbbing of his own heart, often deep and calm but at times overwhelming, intoxicating, setting the soul afire. The momentous reality of God stands there as peace, power, and endless tranquility, as an inexhaustible source of help, as boundless compassion, as an open gate awaiting prayer."[85]

I quote Heschel so frequently because I love the way he speaks and because reading him when I was seventeen and a high school senior was sort of a "white light" experience for me.

Roslyn, New York, where I grew up, is about twenty minutes from Jones Beach. One warm, late spring day in May, just a few weeks before graduation, I cut classes to go to the beach. I liked to get there very early, before eight in the morning, to have the beach all to myself.

Even now, I can still feel the sense of awe I experienced that morning as I sat on the sand, fifty feet from the Atlantic Ocean, seagulls wheeling overhead against a flawless blue sky, the air clean and delicious and just chilly enough to dissuade me from diving into the surf.

I was alone, and I'd brought with me a copy of one of Heschel's books. As I read those consciousness-exploding words of Heschel's, I had the sudden flash that I really knew what he was talking about.

Judaism sees God as a parent, a ruler, but above all as a close, beloved friend, who seeks us out, who wants our company, who asks for our attention. If we perceive God as distant, then God will appear distant. If we choose, however, to see God in the natural world around us, in the love we give others and that others give us, in the inexplicable workings of our miraculous human bodies—if we just once allow ourselves to experience the nearness of God, we will never be the same.

As I sat on the beach and looked around, it was as though my eyes had just been opened. I looked up from the words on the page of *God in Search of Man* and felt God in search of this seventeen-year-old boy. It would take me many years to come to grips with the anger I felt for all the things for which I blamed God, but the Bible tells us that God is patient. I hated God with all my heart for deserting me and for letting my grandfather die and for all the other things that had happened, but God waits for us. On that sunny May morning at Jones Beach, I didn't turn into a God-freak or a religious fanatic. I simply looked back and forth between Heschel's words and God's world, as if I were a tourist consulting a guidebook in a foreign country. And suddenly I knew that God was.

I treasure that moment on the beach, which I have never mentioned to anyone until now, because for the first time in my young life I felt God's presence, God's nearness. And I took a Jewish Scriptures class at college that fall, and I went to a yeshiva for about a year after I graduated college, where I learned to read Hebrew and received an introduction, however basic, to the Talmud and the Bible and Jewish history and Jewish thought. And I've struggled to find the right way to express my sense of God, and my spirituality has waxed and waned. But I'm still here, and still as much a believer as the day I sat on Jones Beach reading Abraham Joshua Heschel, finding God in that fine blue line where the ocean touches the sky; and when I truly understood—or at least I think I understood—what Heschel meant when he quoted the Talmud as saying that there are times when heaven and earth kiss. And that time is when we make the decision to move from God as a taker to God as a giver, from doubt to faith, from suffering God's absence to feeling God's presence.

I felt the kiss that day; and in writing this book, I've only wanted to do one thing—to pass it on to you.

God bless you and keep you, and may you bless and keep God.

10

Now What?

Before we go, two stories.

A young rabbi, fresh from the seminary, gives his first sermon to his new congregation. The topic: keeping kosher.

The next week, half the congregation stays away.

Undaunted, the rabbi gives his second sermon: the importance of observing the Sabbath.

The following week, three quarters of the congregation stays away.

Shaken, the rabbi gives his third sermon: on the importance of avoiding intermarriage.

The following week, only a dozen congregants show up.

Near tears, the young rabbi turns to the president of the congregation, the man who hired him. "What am I doing wrong?" he asks sadly. "Every time I open my mouth, I drive people away."

The president comforts him. "You're doing fine," he says. "But in your next sermon, just talk about *Judaism*."

The second story comes from a book called *Holy Days*. Its author, Lis Harris, spent a year living with the Lubavitch community in Crown Heights, Brooklyn. She asked a rabbi why Judaism couldn't be more flexible in certain areas. The rabbi, she says, responded this way:

"[A] little boy...was playing chess with his father. The father had just set up the chessboard, and the little boy said to him, 'Why must the board always be just like that? Why couldn't we move the kings and rooks over here, and the pawns over there?' And the father answered, 'We could do those things, but then the game wouldn't be chess anymore.'"[86]

I've tried to avoid in the course of this book the question of Jewish practice. I've done this because there are enough excellent books out there that describe how to keep this holiday or how best to observe that commandment. I don't advocate a Judaism devoid of ritual practice or Sabbath or holiday observance; I simply wanted to address the underlying issue of belief.

The traditional attitude in Judaism has always been, "tell us what to do and we'll do it." That attitude only works when people have some reason for belief—either they see their parents, or their peers, or their entire community acting in a certain way. But most Jews today need explanations first. In our times, it's necessary to begin with the question of "Why do we do this?" before we get to the question of "*How* do we do this?" This is a book about Why. I certainly hope that it leads you to books about How.

This book has only touched on the beauty and greatness and spiritual depth of the heritage that every Jew owns. Where you go next is up to you, and I wish you an exciting and challenging spiritual journey, and I hope our spiritual paths cross at some time soon.

It's all waiting for you.

Author's Note

First things first. Bernard Scharfstein, the President of Ktav Publishing House, gave me my start as an author, and I will always be grateful to him. He's had faith in me from the beginning of my career, and I certainly hope that this new book justifies that faith.

Yaakov Elman is a great scholar and a great friend. If this book has any merit at all, it's because he put two years of hard work into it. Yaakov went line by line over six separate drafts of this book and made literally hundreds of suggestions to improve the tone, the accuracy, and the usefulness of the book. He was the best possible editor for this project—or for any project.

Thanks are due also to Bob Milch, who pored over the manuscript as a copy editor and made dozens of suggestions and corrections that made the book much tighter and stronger. Of course, any remaining inaccuracies are strictly the responsibility of the author.

A lot of individuals gave a lot of time to make this project happen. Irving Rosen was extremely helpful in distributing the initial surveys, and I'd like to thank him and all the kind people who answered my questions.

Christine Dargelis did an enormous amount of work checking every single citation in the book. She also helped me by pointing out where my logic or my sentence structure was uneven, and she also did a great job of making sure I explained references that readers might not have understood.

Andrea Hamel and Jennifer Burger also proofread, checked cites, went over the manuscript again and again, and much more, and I want to express my gratitude to them, as well as to Denah Stilerman for the final proofreading.

A number of wonderful people read early drafts and gave me extremely valuable suggestions and comments. They are: Danny Landes and Cheryl Robbins, Susan and Ted Sheftel, Leah Sokoloff, and Irving Rosen. To them I offer my thanks.

An extra special thank you to the staff of the Boston Atheneum, to Catherine Ponder, and to the Kehillat Israel Synagogue in Brookline, Massachusetts, which graciously allowed me free run of their excellent library.

On a personal level, I want to add one thought about how it feels to complete a work like this. I'm certainly experiencing the elation (and exhaustion) that comes from finishing a project this complex. But there's another feeling that I want to note—a sense of profound sadness. How can you really write a book about God? How can you reach conclusions about Jewish theology, history, mysticism, and sociology when you're an expert in none of these fields? Of course you can't. I wrote this book out of a sense of love for the subject and awareness of the crisis currently facing Judaism. I provided extensive footnotes to indicate that I'm not speaking strictly from my own opinions.

I let go of the manuscript with great misgivings: I know how much I've gotten wrong.

But in another sense, that doesn't even matter. This book is meant to be a starting point, an awakening, a presentation of ideas that the reader might not have seen elsewhere. I beg your forgiveness of this book's limitations—and mine. I hope that you find it useful, and thank you for hearing me out.

Michael Graubart Levin
Santa Monica, California
August, 1996
Elul, 5766

Notes

[1] Neil C. Sandberg, *Jewish Life in Los Angeles: A Window to Tomorrow* (Lanham, Md.: University Press of America, 1986), p. 91.

[2] Micah 6:8.

[3] Paul Johnson, *A History of the Jews* (New York: Harper & Row, 1987), pp.133-135.

[4] Ibid., p. 210.

[5] Karen A. Armstrong, *A History of God: The 4000-Year Quest of Judaism, Christianity, and Islam* (New York: Alfred A. Knopf, 1994), p. 357.

[6] Deuteronomy 30:15.

[7] Eliezer Berkovits, *God, Man and History: A Jewish Interpretation* (New York: Jonathan David, 1959), pp. 79-80.

[8] Berkovits, *Faith After the Holocaust*, p. 7.

[9] Ibid., p. 136.

[10] Isaiah 55:8.

[11] Genesis 18:23-32.

[12] Gibran's book *The Prophet*, which has been reprinted many, many times since its initial publication by Knopf in 1923, was, in many ways, the Bible of the 1960s-era counterculture.

[13] David J. Wolpe, *Teaching Your Children About God: A Modern Jewish Approach* (New York: Henry Holt, 1993), p. 74.

[14]Kaufmann, *The Religion of Israel: From Its Beginnings to the Babylonian Exile*, trans. and abridged by Moshe Greenberg (Chicago: University of Chicago Press, 1960), p. 208.

[15]Abraham Joshua Heschel, *God in Search of Man: A Philosophy of Judaism* (New York: Meridian Books, 1995), p. 198.

[16]Whenever I think about the six days of creation, I remember reading *Inherit the Wind* in high school. In it one of the lawyers asks, "Was it a twenty-four-hour day?...There wasn't any sun. How do you know how long it was? Isn't it possible that first day was twenty-five hours long? There was no way to measure it, no way to tell!...It could have been thirty hours! Or a month! Or a hundred years! Or a year! Or ten million years!"

[17]Heschel, *God in Search of Man*, p. 238.

[18]Kaufmann, *Religion of Israel*, p. 12.

[19]Genesis 22:13.

[20]Wolpe, *Teaching Your Children About God*, p. 74.

[21]Heschel, *God in Search of Man*, pp. 270-271.

[22]Ibid., p. 233.

[23]This idea dates back to the twelfth century and Judah Halevi's *Kuzari*.

[24]Exodus 19:16-18, with a midrashic explanation from the Babylonian Talmud, Shabbat 88a.

[25]Kaufmann, *Religion of Israel*, p. 29.

[26]Abraham Joshua Heschel, *The Prophets* (New York: Harper & Row, 1962), p. 22.

[27]Exodus 19:6.

[28]Kaufmann, *Religion of Israel*, p. 87.

[29]Numbers 11:29.

[30]Kaufmann, *Religion of Israel*, p. 121.

[31]Babylonian Talmud, Megillah 14a.

[32]Isaiah 42:6, 49:6.

[33]*Webster's New World Dictionary*, Second College Edition (New York: World, 1976), p. 942.

[34]Gershom S. Scholem, *Sabbatai Sevi: The Mystical Messiah, 1626-1676*, Bollingen Series XVIII (Princeton: Princeton University Press, 1973), p. 15.

[35]I am very grateful to the late Aryeh Kaplan for his *Jewish Meditation: A Practical Guide* (New York: Schocken Books, 1985). My approach to Kabbalah and prayer in the next few paragraphs is based upon his discussion on pp. 132-139.

[36]Gershom Scholem, *On the Mystical Shape of the Godhead*, trans. Joachim Neugroschel, ed. Jonathan Chipman (New York: Schocken Books, 1991), pp. 76-87.

[37]Karen Armstrong, *History of God*, (New York: Knopf, 1994), p. 265.

[38]Ibid., pp. 266-267.

[39]See Genesis 49:10.

[40]See, *e.g.*, Isaiah 43:1, 44:22-23; 48:20; 52:9.

[41]Daniel 12:2-3.

[42]Kaufmann, *Religion of Israel*, pp. 311-312; references to supporting Biblical verses omitted.

[43]II Samuel 28:3-11.

[44]*Kuzari*, p. 80.

[45]Sanhedrin 10:1.

[46]Avot 2:9.

[47]Avot 2:21.

[48]Avot 3:1.

[49]Avot 4:21.

[50]Avot 4:22.

[51]See generally, Saadia Gaon, *Book of Beliefs and Opinions*, trans. S. Rosenblatt (New Haven: Yale University Press, 1948).

[52]Greenstone, *The Messianic Idea in Jewish History*, (Westport, CT: Greenwood Press), p. 128.

[53]Maimonides lived in Egypt, an Islamic country, and under Islam Jews were forbidden to ride horses because a Jew astride a horse would be in a higher position than a Muslim pedestrian.

[54]Some Christians consider it a religious duty to convert not just Jews but everyone to Christianity; that's another matter altogether.

[55]*Journal of Reform Judaism*, Winter 1989, p. 19.

[56]Mark Lee Raphael, Profiles in American Judaism (New York: Harper & Row, 1984), p. 66.

[57]Elliot Strom, "Where Is the Awe?" *Journal of Reform Judaism*, Winter 1989, p. 11.

[58]Jack Wertheimer, *A People Divided: Judaism in Contemporary America* (New York: Basic Books, 1993), p. 63.

[59]Neil Sandberg, *Jewish Life in Los Angeles: A Window to Tomorrow* (Lanham, Maryland: University Press of America, 1986), p. 22.

[60]Ibid., p. 23.

[61]Sidney Godstein, "Profile of American Jewry," American Jewish Yearbook (1992), p. 92.

[62]Marshall Sklare, *Conservative Judaism: An American Religious Movement* (New York: Schocken Books, 1972), p. 228.

[63]Helen Jeiven, *Checklist for a Perfect Bar Mitzvah* (Garden City, N.Y.: Doubleday, 1983), p. 2.

[64]Ibid., p. 40.

[65]Sylvan D. Schwartzman, *Reform Judaism in the Making* (New York: Union of American Hebrew Congregations, 1962), p. 9.

[66]Wertheimer, *People Divided*, p. 38, quoting the newspaper of Agudath Israel, an Orthodox organization.

[67]Ibid., p. 178.

[68]Sklare, *Conservative Judaism*, p. 265.

[69]Eli Ginsberg, *Agenda for America's Jews* (New York: King's Crown Press, 1950), p. 13.

[70]Pinchas Peli, *Soloveitchik on Repentance* (New York: Paulist Press, 1984), p. 181.

[71]See David Landau's excellent book, *Piety and Power: The World of Jewish Fundamentalism* (New York: Hill & Wang, 1993), p. 292, for a discussion of this phenomenon.

[72]Nosson Scherman, "An Overview: Destruction and Redemption," in *Megillas Eichah, Lamentations: A New Translation*, trans. and compiled by Meir Zlotowitz (Brooklyn, N.Y.: Mesorah, 1978), p. xxxv.

[73]Heschel, *God in Search of Man*, p. 31.

[74]Mishnah Peah 1:1.

[75]Hertzberg, *Being Jewish in America: The Modern Experience* (New York: Schocken, 1979), p. xiv.

[76]See, for example, Isaiah 6:2, Ezekiel 10:5.

[77]See the end of Kiddushin in the Jerusalem Talmud.

[78]Heschel, *God in Search of Man*, p. 264.

[79]See Exodus 21:10 and commentaries thereon.

[80]See Talmud Yuma 13a-b.

[81]Rabbi Harold Schulweis, a leading Conservative thinker, coined the term "predicate theology" for the worldview of those who do not accept the idea that there is a God but still want to concern themselves with the idea of godliness-of acting the way God would act if there were a God. See the discussion in Leonard Fein, *Where Are We?* (New York: Harper & Row, 1988), p. 27.

[82]Heschel, *Prophets*, p. 22.

[83]Heschel, *God in Search of Man*, p. 98.

[84]Kaplan, *Jewish Meditation*, p. 92.

[85]Heschel, *God in Search of Man*, p. 282.

[86]Lis Harris, *Holy Days*